W. E. B. Du Bois

The Library of African American Biography
General Editor: John David Smith
Charles H. Stone Distinguished Professor of American History
University of North Carolina at Charlotte

The Library of African American Biography aims to provide concise, readable, and up-to-date lives of leading black figures in American history, in widely varying fields of accomplishment. The books are written by accomplished scholars and writers, and reflect the most recent historical research and critical interpretation. Illustrated with photographs, they are designed for general informed readers as well as for students.

Titles in the Series

W. E. B. Du Bois: An American Intellectual and Activist, by Shawn Leigh Alexander (2015)
Paul Robeson: A Life of Activism and Art, by Lindsey R. Swindall (2013)
Ella Baker: Community Organizer of the Civil Rights Movement, by J. Todd Moye (2013)
Booker T. Washington: Black Leadership in the Age of Jim Crow, by Raymond W. Smock (2010)
Walter White: The Dilemma of Black Identity in America, by Thomas Dyja (2010)
Richard Wright: From Black Boy to World Citizen, by Jennifer Jensen Wallach (2010)
Louis Armstrong: The Soundtrack of the American Experience, by David Stricklin (2010)

W. E. B. Du Bois

An American Intellectual and Activist

Shawn Leigh Alexander

ROWMAN & LITTLEFIELD
Lanham • Boulder • New York • London

Published by Rowman & Littlefield
A wholly owned subsidiary of The Rowman & Littlefield Publishing Group, Inc.
4501 Forbes Boulevard, Suite 200, Lanham, Maryland 20706
www.rowman.com

Unit A, Whitacre Mews, 26-34 Stannary Street, London SE11 4AB

British Library Cataloguing in Publication Information Available

Library of Congress Cataloging-in-Publication Data Available

Alexander, Shawn Leigh.
W. E. B. Du Bois : an American intellectual and actvist / by Shawn Leigh Alexander.
p. cm.
Includes bibliographical references and index.
ISBN 978-1-4422-0740-0 (cloth : alk. paper) -- ISBN 978-1-4422-0742-4 (electronic)

∞ ™ The paper used in this publication meets the minimum requirements of American National Standard for Information Sciences Permanence of Paper for Printed Library Materials, ANSI/NISO Z39.48-1992.

Printed in the United States of America

Contents

Preface   vii

Acknowledgments   xi

1   The Early Years   1

2   The Study of the Negro   17

3   Of Du Bois, Booker T. Washington, and Others: A Challenge of Leadership   35

4   Building Movement: The NAACP, Pan-Africanism, Garvey, and a Renaissance   59

5   The Wings of Atlanta and the NAACP Redux   85

6   Marching toward Peace   111

A Note on Sources   133

Index   145

About the Author   155

Preface

In the folds of this European civilization I was born and shall die, imprisoned, conditioned, depressed, exalted and inspired. Integrally a part of it and yet, much more significant, one of its rejected parts. . . . Crucified on the vast wheel of time, I flew round and round the Zeitgeist, waving my pen and lifting faint voices to explain, expound and exhort; to see, foresee and prophesy, to the few who would listen.

—W. E. B. Du Bois, 1940

To tackle a short, accessible biography of William Edward Burghardt Du Bois fifty years after his death is a daunting endeavor. Despite his ineradicable presence in American and international history, and numerous academic pages written about his activism and intellectual brilliance, the vast majority of Americans still have little knowledge of the man, his thought, or his actions. *W. E. B. Du Bois: An American Intellectual and Activist* is a primer into the world and writings of W. E. B. Du Bois. He was an extraordinay author who published twenty books of poetry, literature, and social, historical, economic, and political inquiry, the majority of which appeared in the final third of his life. In addition, he gave countless addresses, wrote hundreds of newspaper columns, edited a number of academic and popular journals, and helped form and actively participated in many civil rights organizations. Since his death in 1963, there have been more than forty primary source anthologies of his work, the majority published after his vast manuscript collection was donated to the University of Massachusetts-Amherst and made available to the public. Further, more than twenty scholarly anthologies have been published on Du Bois and the significance of his life and work. Finally, since the publication of Francis Broderick's *W. E. B. Du Bois, Negro Leader in a Time of Crisis* (1959), there has been more than twenty scholarly biographies written on Du Bois and his intellectual thought. With all of these pages written by and about Du Bois it is easy to understand that he is one of the greatest intellectuals and activists to write, speak, teach, and lecture in America. As Meyer Weinberg declared, "If the intellectual is a tensor between scholarship and social action, Du Bois fulfilled the role with the highest distinction." Moreover, Du Bois was a global citizen. He was always a scholar and activist that thought beyond the borders of the United States, recognizing the international aspects of color and class in the struggles of the darker peoples of the world. In 1953, when he was asked whether he still subscribed to the prophetic idea he professed in 1903 that "the problem of the twentieth century is the problem of the color line," Du Bois wrote:

> I still think today as yesterday that the color line is a great problem of this century. But today I see more clearly than yesterday that back of the problem of race and color, lies a greater problem which both obscures and implements it; and that is the fact that so many civilized persons are willing to live in comfort even if the price of this is poverty, ignorance and disease of the majority of their fellow men; that to maintain this privilege men have waged war until today war tends to become universal and continuous, and the excuse for this war continues largely to be color and race.

Du Bois was born in Great Barrington, Massachusetts, in 1868 and died in Ghana in 1963. He studied at Fisk University and the University of Berlin and was the first black Ph.D. from Harvard (1895). With the influence of his graduate studies in Germany, Du Bois was one of the founders of sociology, publishing the still-significant sociological treatise *The Philadelphia Negro* in 1899. He helped establish the now-over-a-century-old civil rights organization the National Association for the Advancement of Colored People (NAACP). From 1910 to 1934 he served as director of publicity and research for the organization, as well as editor of its important journal, *The Crisis*. After a split and absence from the leadership of the group Du Bois returned as the director of special research from 1944 to 1948. During these two phases with the NAACP, in addition to his editorial duties, he was a leader, in voice and action, in the fight against racial discrimination and violence, as well as world conflict.

Du Bois was also an influential architect of the Harlem Renaissance in his role with *The Crisis* and as an active participatory writer of both fiction and nonfiction works during the period. Additionally, he was a world leader of Pan-Africanism, serving in 1900 as secretary of the first Pan-African Conference. He was also a leading participant in the Pan-African Congresses of 1919, 1921, 1923, and 1945. His interest in the plight of Africans throughout the world led him to be a pioneer in the study of Africa and the Diaspora and ultimately the conception of the *Encyclopedia Africana*, a comprehensive history of the Diaspora. Finally, during the last decade and a half of his life, Du Bois became deeply involved with world peace and was a staunch opponent of the use of nuclear weapons.

W. E. B. Du Bois: An American Intellectual and Activist tells this story in a clear and concise manner. It explores Du Bois's racial strategy, civil rights activity, journalistic career, and his role as an international spokesman. The biography also captures his life as a historian, sociologist, artist, propagandist, and activist. Additionally, it places him in context with his chief critics—among others, Booker T. Washington, Marcus Garvey, Walter White, as well as the federal government after World War II.

W. E. B. Du Bois: An American Intellectual and Activist begins the reader's journey toward discovering who the brilliant and complicated Du Bois was. As anthropologist St. Clair Drake said, "His was a life 'experimentally lived and self-documented'—a restless seeking, ever-searching quest, a life of journey which began in New England, carried him over the whole world, and ended—by his own choice—on the Guinea Coast." But above all, as Du Bois himself wrote in 1952, he was "a citizen of the world as well as the United States of America" and claimed as such to have "the right to know and think and tell the truth as he saw it." He despised "men and nations which judge human beings by their color, religious beliefs or income." He was also an individual who believed in the world that he, his peers, and we, the future generations, were, and are, creating. He had a deep concern for the life of future generations—generations that he wanted to live in a world that did not know the veil of color prejudice, the costs of war, or the sting of inequality. In essence, he was always trying to make the world a better place, a more righteous place, a more just place. As author John Oliver Killens stated, Du Bois had "run a tremendous race, and now it would be up to us, all of us everywhere, to take the torch and carry it forward. He has left us a legacy of scholarship and struggle."

Acknowledgments

Researching and writing this book has been time-consuming, intimidating, occasionally frustrating, and constantly challenging and rewarding. I am greatly indebted to John David Smith, who first contacted me about writing this book over a decade ago. As his series continued to grow, he would occasionally contact me, simply stating, "I would like you to write the Du Bois biography when you are ready." I do not know if anyone is ever ready to write a concise biography of W. E. B. Du Bois, but I am deeply thankful to John David for his tenacity and for giving me this opportunity. Without his advice, assistance, and perseverance this book would not have been realized.

Like many scholars of the African American experience, I was first introduced to Du Bois when I read the beautiful and mesmerizing *The Souls of Black Folk*, but my real investigation into the writings and intellectual thought of Du Bois began at the University of Massachusetts-Amherst. While a graduate student in the W. E. B. Du Bois Department of Afro-American Studies, through courses and discussions with Ernest Allen Jr., John H. Bracey, and David W. Blight, as well as William Strickland, Julius Lester, and David Graham Du Bois, I discovered the complexity, insightfulness, and scope of Du Bois's thoughts and actions. I am indebted to the conversations that I had with these scholars and the hours I spent in the archives at the W. E. B. Du Bois Library at UMass. I also wish to acknowledge my indebtedness to the great body of scholarship on Du Bois, and African American history in general, on which this biography rests, and work produced over the past several generations by scholars such as Herbert Aptheker, Gerald Horne, David Levering Lewis, Leon Litwack, Manning Marable, August Meier, Wilson J. Moses, Elliott Rudwick, Eric Sundquist, William Tuttle, and Raymond Wolters. The interpretations of broad issues in this book owe much to their work.

So many individuals have generously contributed their thoughtful suggestions, it would be impossible to name them all. I am grateful to David W. Blight, John H. Bracey, Ernest Allen Jr., Jonathan Earle, Jeffery Moran, David Goldberg, William Tuttle, Randal Jelks, and Dave Tell, for their comments, critical advice, and willingness to listen to the details of the life of this incredible American intellectual and activist. Clarence Lang and Jacob Dorman deserve special mention, not only for their support and guidance, but also their willingness to read and offer valuable suggestions on the complete manuscript at a crucial juncture. In addition, I appreciate the intellectual exchange I have enjoyed with my other colleagues at the University of Kansas and the Department of African and African-American Studies as I wrote and refined this biography. This book is much better for all of their suggestions and contributions. I would also like to thank J&S Coffee for the bottomless cups and the Lawrence Leftist Circle—Gary, Frank, Chuck, Ken, Paul, and Paul—for their conversation and often-needed distraction.

Additionally, I owe a special debt to John David Smith for his close reading of the book and his keen observations and sage advice along the way. I am also thankful to the editors at Rowman & Littlefield who fostered this manuscript through the process of publication. Particularly I would like to express my sincere appreciation to Jon Sisk who remained enthusiastic and patient throughout the whole process.

Finally, I want to dedicate this book to my family. Leigham and Francis, you bring me joy, and of course a bit of frustration, every day, but I cannot imagine my life without the two of you greeting me as I walk through the door each evening. Above all else, I deeply thank my best friend and spouse, Kelly Marie Farrell. It is not easy to explain gratitude for the most important person in your life, especially when she is vital to both your work and your personal happiness. She has given me everything: love, support, companionship, therapy, and nourishment, all without the same unselfishness reciprocated. I thank you for everything you do. I hope one day I can become as strong an individual as you demonstrate every day.

Lawrence, Kansas

December 15, 2014

Chapter One

The Early Years

My boyhood seems, if my memory serves me rightly, to have been filled with incidents of surprisingly little importance. . . . In early youth a great bitterness entered my life and kindled a great ambition. I wanted to go to college because others did. I came and graduated and am now in search of a Ph.D. and bread. I believe, foolishly perhaps but sincerely, that I have something to say to the world.

—W. E. B. Du Bois, 1890

On August 28, 1963, as nearly one-quarter of a million people gathered on a bright, sunny day in Washington, D.C., for the historic March on Washington for Jobs and Freedom, word came across the Atlantic that William Edward Burghardt Du Bois had died the previous day in Accra, Ghana. Those in attendance paused for a moment of veneration for one of the leading intellectuals and activists of the twentieth century. Roy Wilkins, the executive secretary of the National Association for the Advancement of Colored People, told those in attendance to "remember, this has been a long fight. . . . [and] it is incontrovertible that at the dawn of the twentieth century his was the voice that was calling to you to gather here today in this great cause. If you want to read something that applies to 1963," he continued, "go back and get a volume of *The Souls of Black Folk* by Du Bois published in 1903."

Dr. Du Bois had lived to the age of ninety-five and was an active voice in the African American community for eighty-two of those years. He molded the lives and minds of so many within and without the black community with his words and actions. Horace Mann Bond, African American educator and activist and father of Julian Bond, former Student Nonviolent Coordinating

1

Committee activist and executive director of the NAACP, explained, "Through *The Crisis* Du Bois helped shape my inner world to a degree impossible to imagine in the world of contemporary children, and the flood of various mass media to which they are exposed. . . . through Du Bois I had these vicarious experiences with the real and brutal world of race and color, as with the real world of black men and women clothed in beauty and dignity." Langston Hughes echoed Bond as he stated, "So many thousands of my generation were uplifted and inspired by the written and spoken words of Dr. W. E. B. Du Bois that for me to say I was so inspired would hardly be unusual. My earliest memories of written words are of those of Du Bois and the Bible." Moreover, as civil rights and labor activist James E. Jackson explained, "What Emerson said of John Brown can be said with equal justice of W. E. B. Du Bois: 'He was the most ideal of men, for he wanted to put all his ideas into action.'"

Amid all the praise upon his death, however, Du Bois was also vilified. Throughout the first half of the twentieth century, to some blacks and whites, he was a malevolent man who should be incarcerated, ostracized, or deported. In 1919, South Carolina congressman James F. Byrnes from the floor of the House of Representatives accused him of sedition. In 1934, after Du Bois resigned from the NAACP and *The Crisis*, Arthur C. Macneal, president of the Chicago branch of the organization, declared that the sixty-six-year-old activist was worse than Benedict Arnold and should be relegated to the same "fate if a worse one cannot be made." Most scathingly, Du Bois's nemesis Marcus Garvey, the leader of the Universal Negro Improvement Association, dismissed the NAACP leader as "purely and simply a white man's nigger." Who was this man of great influence and intellect, who not only wanted to "understand the world" but was committed to the task of "changing the world of men so that men would be to man as a brother and not as a beast"?

William Edward Burghardt Du Bois was born February 23, 1868, to Mary Burghardt and Alfred Du Bois in Great Barrington, Massachusetts, a town "of middle class people" and according to Du Bois "a boy's paradise. There were mountains to climb and rivers to wade and swim. . . . My earlier contacts with playmates and other human beings were normal and pleasant." To Du Bois, however, the location of his birth "was less important than" his "birth time." He was born days after Thaddeus Stevens, radical Republican

Figure 1.1. Great Barrington, Massachusetts—W. E. B. Du Bois as a baby in the arms of his mother, spring 1868. Courtesy University of Massachusetts Archives.

senator, gave his final impassioned speech on the floor calling for the impeachment of Andrew Johnson. That same year the Fourteenth Amendment was ratified, allowing blacks to vote and take part in government rewriting of state constitutions in the South and helping elect former Union commander Ulysses S. Grant as president of the United States.

In addition to the portentous time of his birth, the rich ancestral histories of the families he was born into exhibited the distinctiveness of the Afro-American world that developed in the Western Hemisphere. Du Bois's maternal great-grandfather was a West African slave, born in the 1730s, who was brought to western Massachusetts and gained manumission after the Revolutionary War. His paternal grandfather was descended from French Huguenots who immigrated to New York and then to the Bahamas, and was born in Haiti. The Burghardt Du Bois ancestral roots were therefore African, Caribbean, African American, North American, Dutch, and French. Or as Du Bois was fond of saying, he was born "with a flood of Negro blood, a strain of French, a bit of Dutch, but thank God! No Anglo-Saxon."

Du Bois never knew his father. The explanation he offered varied throughout his life. In *Dusk of Dawn*, his first autobiography, he explained that his father died when he was an infant. Later, in his final autobiography, he stated that his father left, a short time before his birth, "to establish a home for his family" in New Milford, Connecticut. According to this account, his father wrote Mary asking her to join him, but her parents objected and she remained in Great Barrington to raise their son.

Growing up in the picturesque Massachusetts Berkshires in the wake of emancipation, Du Bois experienced a color line, but it was not rigid. In Great Barrington, a town of five thousand with a small African American population, he grew up feeling "no sense of difference or separation from the main mass of towns people." Blacks "congregated together in their own social life . . . because that was the rule in the town," not because of a Jim Crow system that was growing in the southern states or even the de facto and de jure segregation that existed in other northern areas.

Du Bois excelled in his favorite subjects in school and felt respected by his peers and teachers. As the young budding scholar explained, "I found it easy to excel most of my classmates in studies if not in games. The secret of life and the loosing of the color bar, then, lay in excellence, in accomplishment. If others of my family, of my colored kin, had stayed in school instead of quitting early for small jobs, they could have risen to equal whites. On this my mother quietly insisted. There was no real discrimination on account of color—it was all a matter of ability and hard work."

Eventually, he did "discover" he was black and therefore vulnerable, unable to defeat everyone's prejudice with "hard work." The discovery occurred in the innocent schoolyard when a peer showed racist disdain toward the young Du Bois. As he explained years later in his 1903 landmark collection, *The Souls of Black Folk*:

> Something put it into the boys' and girls' heads to buy gorgeous visiting cards—ten cents a package—and exchange. The exchange was merry, till one girl, a tall newcomer, refused my card,—refused it peremptorily, with a glance. Then it dawned upon me with a certain suddenness that I was different from the others . . . shut out from the white world by a vast veil.

In addition to this experience, he had heard the older Burghardts speak of race and racial injustice; moreover, he had personally felt the sting of racial prejudice from some children of Irish immigrants. As he explained, "I was afraid of the Irish and kept away from their part of town as much as possible. Sometimes they called me 'nigger' or tried to attack me."

Despite the burn of racial prejudice befalling him from time to time in Great Barrington, his mother's words were his guiding light to survive. The young Du Bois exhibited respectability, demonstrating his worth and humanity to those around him through his moral virtue, proper speech, appearance, and above all his skill and intelligence. As he explained, "If visitors to school saw and remarked on my brown face, I waited in quiet confidence. When my turn came, I recited glibly and usually correctly because I studied hard. . . . I gave the best a hard run, and then sat back complacently."

This work ethic drove the young Du Bois and would continue to drive his long life as an activist, scholar, and social commentator. His public life began earlier than most. When he was fifteen, he became the Great Barrington correspondent for the *New York Globe*, a black newspaper edited by T. Thomas Fortune, one of the leading intellectuals and activists of the late nineteenth and early twentieth centuries. The *Globe* had a number of community columns from cities and towns in the East, which reported the social and cultural life of blacks in the area. Du Bois's columns, twenty-seven from April 14, 1883, to May 16, 1885, offer an excellent picture of the social life of the time and hint at Du Bois's developing racial consciousness and political outlook.

The July 12, 1884, issue of the *Globe* carried news of Great Barrington's high school graduation, including the graduation of a young Du Bois and his successful address on the abolitionist Wendell Phillips, who had died the previous February. Du Bois would later state that he was "fascinated by his life and his work" and that by researching Phillips's life for his graduation speech, he "took a long step toward a wider conception of what" he was "going to do."

The young graduate had high ambitions. It was less than common for students, white or black, to go to college in 1884. While less than 5 percent of the college-age population would continue into higher education in the 1880s, Du Bois and many of the townspeople understood he could succeed and ought to pursue a postsecondary education. His movement toward higher education, however, was delayed by the death of his mother in the fall of 1884. Penniless and orphaned, the teenage graduate worked for a year and studied before he left home, traveling south to Tennessee and Fisk University, a school founded shortly after the Civil War by the American Mission-

Figure 1.2. Great Barrington, Massachusetts. High school graduating class, June 1884. W. E. B. Du Bois, "Willie." Courtesy University of Massachusetts Archives.

ary Association "to establish for the colored people of the South a University" that would create leaders "in vitally important work that needs to be done for their race in this country and on the continent of Africa."

Though the budding scholar was interested in attending Harvard College, the group of Congregational churches that each pledged $25 for four years to finance Du Bois's education believed that Fisk, a southern Congregational school for blacks, would better suit Du Bois as a young black man. Members of his family were not pleased with the idea of sending the young Du Bois to the South. As he explained, "They said frankly that . . . I was Northern born and bred and instead of preparing me for work and giving me an opportunity right there in my own town and state, [the white benefactors] were bundling me off to the South."

While surely frustrated about his inability to attend Harvard, Du Bois himself was interested in leaving the North.

> I was beginning to feel lonesome in New England. Unconsciously, I realized that as I grew older, and especially now that I had finished the public school, the close cordial intermingling with my white fellows would grow more restricted. There would be meetings, parties, clubs, to which I would not be invited. Especially in the case of strangers, visitors, newcomers to the town would my presence and friendship become a matter of explanation or even embarrassment to my schoolmates.

Moreover, around the same time, he was becoming aware of the "spiritual isolation" in which he was living. A few months before leaving for the South, he had traveled to visit his paternal grandfather in New Bedford, Massachusetts. On the way home he stopped at "the annual picnic at Rocky Point on Narragansett Bay where colored people of three states were wont to assemble." The experience left a lasting impression on Du Bois, as he saw "in open-mouthed astonishment the whole gorgeous gamut of the American Negro world; the swaggering men, the beautiful girls, the laughter and gaiety, the unhampered self-expression." He was ready to experience this world and move away from the racially isolated sphere he lived in, Great Barrington, Massachusetts. Therefore, he was eager to go to Fisk, to go south, "the South of slavery, rebellion and black folk."

This excitement continued when the seventeen-year-old sophomore—his excellent record in high school allowed him to skip his freshman year—arrived in Nashville.

I was thrilled to be for the first time among so many people of my own color or rather of such various and extraordinary colors, which I had only glimpsed before, but who it seemed were bound to me by new and exciting and eternal ties. Never before had I seen young men so self-assured and who gave themselves such airs, and colored men at that; and above all for the first time I saw beautiful girls. At my home among my white school mates there were a few pretty girls; but either they were not entrancing or, because I had known them all my life I did not notice them; but at Fisk at the first dinner I saw opposite me a girl whom I have often said, no human being could possibly have been as beautiful as she seemed to my eyes that far-off September night of 1885.

Being surrounded by African Americans for the first time in his life was exhilarating. The young Du Bois looked around him in wonder. For possibly the first time he sat in utter amazement with his fellow African Americans. The northern-raised Du Bois arrived in the South as part of a black community and became instinctively proud of his race and the blood that "flows in my veins." He wrote to his minister back in Great Barrington that he sometimes sat in wonderment as his two to three hundred companions assembled for morning prayer. "I can hardly realize that they are all my people," he declared, "that this great assembly of youth and intelligence are the representatives of a race which twenty years ago was in bondage . . . it is a bracing thought to know that I stand among those who do not despise me for my color."

Despite being opened to his new community, the young college student did not become immune to American racism and discrimination. In particular while in Nashville he experienced racism and segregation in ways he had never dreamed possible. Tennessee had led the nation in the creation of post–Civil War de jure segregation. In 1870, the state passed a statute against intermarriage, which quickly became the model for every southern state. Again, in 1881, the Volunteer State led the way as it adopted the first Jim Crow law, which segregated African Americans on railroad cars and in depots. After the Supreme Court ruling in 1883 on the Civil Rights Cases, which declared the Civil Rights Act of 1875 unconstitutional, Tennessee, like other states, passed additional Jim Crow laws segregating public and private establishments, including hotels, restaurants, theaters, parks, libraries, and barbershops.

As Du Bois explained, "The public disdain and even insult in race contact on the street continually took my breath." The New Englander needed to make adjustments in his interactions across the color line. He was shocked by the everyday violence of the South and even more astonished to learn that many of his colleagues carried guns as a normal part of their dress. As G. D. Field, a classmate who "knew and hated the white South," told Du Bois, "You don't need [a pistol] often but when you do, it comes in handy!"

Du Bois often told of how he came to know the white South and "the ethics of living Jim Crow." One incident occurred in a Nashville street when he "accidentally jostled a white woman." Upon making contact he, "in accord with my New England training," raised his hat and apologized. He was immediately taken aback by the white woman's response.

> Somehow, I cannot say how, I had transgressed the interracial mores of the South. Was it because I showed no submissiveness? Did I fail to debase myself utterly and eat spiritual dirt? Did I act as equal among equals? I do not know. I only sensed scorn and hate; the kind of despising which a dog might incur. Thereafter, for at least half a century I avoided the necessity of showing them [whites] courtesy of any sort. If I did them any courtesy which sometimes I must in sheer deference to my own standards of decency, I contrived to act as if totally unaware that I saw or had them in mind.

Even though the young, northern-bred Du Bois often experienced racial affronts and had a steep learning curve in negotiating the Jim Crow South, he enjoyed his time at Fisk. As he stated years later, "I was at Harvard but not of it. I was a student of Berlin, but still the son of Fisk." His time in Nashville, according to Du Bois, was a period "of splendid inspiration and nearly perfect happiness, under teachers whom I respected and amid surroundings that inspired me." The faculty, nearly all white, "believe[d] in the possibilities of the Negro race" and unlike other southern schools created in the wake of the Civil War, did not focus on industrial education, training laborers for the white South; rather the curriculum was designed to train Du Bois and his peers to be leaders of the race. As Du Bois's biographer David Levering Lewis stated, for Du Bois "Fisk was basic training for combat, and Fiskites were to provide the officer corps. If [Du Bois] had not yet coined this most famous term, the concept of the 'talented tenth' must already have been gestating."

Leadership became a theme that Du Bois and his peers returned to multiple times during his tenure at the school. In an address before his classmates he declared that he was "a Negro, and I glory in the name! I am proud of the black blood that flows in my veins. From all the recollections dear to my boyhood have I come here, not to pose as a critic but to join hands with this, my people."

During two summers of his tenure at Fisk the young Du Bois ventured into the countryside of eastern Tennessee to teach school and gain a greater understanding of southern black rural life. He later wrote that during this period he encountered "the real seat of slavery. . . . I touched intimately the lives of the commonest of mankind—people who ranged from barefoot dwellers on dirt floors, with patched rags for clothes, to rough hard-working farmers, with plain, clean plenty." His school, held in "a log cabin built before the Civil War," was only the second session "held in the district since Emancipation." On a personal level, while in rural Tennessee the young Du Bois also discovered sex when he slept with his landlady, "an unhappy wife."

Du Bois's eyes were opened to more than sex during his summers in rural Tennessee. He discovered black life and labor as well in the warm months among his "people." Frequently, he spent the evenings visiting the families of his students, many of whom were older than he, sitting on porches, eating the fresh seasonal fruits, and talking about life, struggles, and dreams. Among these conversations and during his daily comings and goings Du Bois heard about and witnessed suffering: African Americans segregated in public accommodations, held in debt servitude, denied access to the franchise and the courts, and occasional physically brutalized due to the developing Jim Crow system.

One of his favorite places to visit was the home of his student Josie, "a thin, homely girl of 20," who was later described in the fourth chapter of *The Souls of Black Folk*, "Of the Meaning of Progress." Time seemingly stood still for these folk, he explained. Later he would write that their lives were "dull and humdrum." In his last autobiography Du Bois would argue that the black community was a world made from isolation. "There was among us," he explained, "but a half-awakened common consciousness, sprung from common hardship in poverty, poor land and low wages; and, above all, from the sight of the Veil that hung between us and Opportunity." His time in rural Tennessee helped him to recognize such things, and his understanding would continue to sharpen over time.

Du Bois returned to the ideas of leadership and unification during the summer of 1888 in his graduation address. His subject was German unifier Otto von Bismarck. He later explained that his choice demonstrated "the abyss between my education and the truth of the world. Bismarck was my hero. He had made a nation out of a mass of bickering peoples. . . . This foreshadowed in my mind the kind of thing that American Negroes must do, marching forth with strength and determination under trained leadership. On the other hand, I did not understand at all, nor had my history course led me to understand, anything of current European intrigue, of the expansion of European power into Africa, of the industrial revolution built on slave trade and now turning into colonial imperialism. . . . I was blithely European and imperialist in outlook; democratic as democracy was conceived in America."

So with this significant but innocent political outlook, Du Bois left Fisk, and the South, to enter Harvard College as a junior. The school had deemed his Fisk degree inadequate for admission to graduate school. While in Cambridge, his personal life was lonely and difficult. He returned to New England with "the theory of race separation . . . quite" in his blood. Assuming that Harvard's students were preparing themselves "for different careers in worlds largely different," and "following the attitudes which [he] had adopted in the South," Du Bois "did not seek contact" with his "white fellow students. On the whole rather avoided them."

While he did not seek acquaintances in the white community, Du Bois did make contacts in black Boston. In particular he became a friend and regular at the home of Josephine Ruffin, an African American journalist, civil rights activist, suffragist, and widow of Judge George Lewis Ruffin, who was the first black graduate of Harvard Law School in 1869. At the Ruffin home on Charles Street Du Bois met many intellectual black Boston Brahmins, in particular a number of women who were excellent theater and travel companions throughout the region. This was not, however, Du Bois's focus while at Harvard. He never neglected his studies; burning "no midnight oil," he was focused on the task at hand. As he explained later, he "asked nothing of Harvard but the tutelage of teachers and the freedom of the library."

Tutelage he did receive. While at Harvard he studied with George Santayana and developed a close relationship with William James, as well as with Albert Bushnell Hart, one of America's leading historians, who took Du Bois under his wing. It was under Hart, who had just returned from Germany with a new methodology of studying and writing history, that Du Bois, as an undergraduate, began the earliest research on his first book, *The Suppression of the African Slave-Trade to the United States of America, 1638-1870* (1896). Hart believed that historians needed to move away from retelling old stories based on secondary sources. He encouraged his students to instead spend more time in the archives with the sources and develop new, well-documented interpretations and analysis. With the encouragement of Hart,

Du Bois started examining the documents of the transatlantic slave trade. While Du Bois majored in philosophy, his experience with Hart led him to history for his graduate field of study. According to Du Bois, Hart "brought me down to earth by making me study documents and look up facts pretty carefully."

He graduated in 1890, cum laude, and because his grades placed him at the top of his class, he again was chosen to speak at his commencement exercises. On this occasion he chose to speak on Jefferson Davis. "I chose it with deliberate intent of facing Harvard," he would explain, "and the nation with a discussion of slavery as illustrated in person of the president of the Confederate States of America."

After his graduation he immediately entered graduate school, though as he explained, "I did not feel prepared. I felt that to cope with the new and extraordinary situations then developing in the United States and the world, I needed to go further, and that as a matter of fact I had just well begun my training in knowledge of social conditions." He combined the teaching of his

Figure 1.3.   Du Bois in the group of the six speakers at the graduation of 281 Harvard students. Courtesy University of Massachusetts Archives.

two mentors, James and Hart, applying philosophy "to a historical interpretation of race relations." As he later explained, he was making his "first steps toward sociology as the science of human action." Within a year he had finished drafts of his doctoral dissertation, focusing on the suppression of the African slave trade to America. This preliminary research on the trade constituted his master's thesis, which was completed in 1892. Prior to receiving his degree, in December 1891, with the encouragement and assistance of Hart, he presented his research, a paper titled "The Enforcement of the Slave Trade Laws," before the American Historical Association, a society of historians and professors of history in the United States founded in 1884. After completing his master's degree he sought to continue his studies in Europe, specifically Germany, at the University of Berlin.

The financially strapped Du Bois contemplated how he would afford to move across the Atlantic and enroll at Berlin. He sent an application to former President Rutherford B. Hayes, the current chairman of the Slater Fund, after seeing an advertisement for the Slater Fund for the Education of Negroes describing a new program that assisted African Americans in their quest for an education overseas. He was denied the fellowship because, as Hayes explained, the original advertisement was a mistake; there was no such program.

Demonstrating courage for any young college graduate, but particularly a young black graduate in the 1890s, Du Bois immediately penned a protest stating that he really had not believed that the Slater Fund, the group who had used their resources only on "training plowmen," would now fund higher education for blacks overseas. Moreover, he scolded Hayes and the Slater Fund for their tone in the rejection letter and the original advertisement, which gave the impression that no African American had the aptitude for advanced education in art and literature. He concluded that Hayes owed "an apology to the Negro people." Hayes answered by telling the young, ambitious Du Bois to apply again, which he did, and in turn he was rewarded for his efforts, receiving $1,500 for two years of graduate study in Europe.

Even though Du Bois suffered through the tension that cloaked everyday interactions between whites and blacks in Nashville and Boston alike, he reveled in the freedom to have drinks, conversations, and good times with white Europeans without the veil of U.S. racism. Traveling on a steamship toward Germany, he enjoyed the company of a Dutch woman with her two grown daughters. The four passed the time by eating, singing, and speaking English, French, and German together. Du Bois enjoyed his travel companions so much that he shed tears when they went their separate ways. In 1892, when traveling in the summer to the town of Eisenach, he fell in love with blue-eyed Dora Marbach, who wanted to marry "*gleich* [at once]" after he wooed her with his strong serenading one evening. Then while in Berlin he spent many pleasurable evenings with Amalie, a white shop girl. He also palled around with white men, traveling Europe with two fellow students, attending political rallies, and conversing with Germans in restaurants and beer halls.

At the University of Berlin, where Du Bois spent more time studying than socializing when classes were in session, he studied theoretical political economy and industrialism and society under such figures as economists Adolf Wagner and Gustav Schmoller; historian Heinrich von Treitschke; and sociologist, philosopher, and political economist Max Weber. While studying under these exceptional scholars, Du Bois was introduced to an interdisciplinary field of study, orchestrated greatly by Wagner and Schmoller, known as *Staatswissenschaften*, where insights were drawn from diverse areas such as economics, statistics, sociology, history, and public administration. All his instructors encouraged him to use this more interdisciplinary, inductive method rather than rely on a more deductive, theoretical approach to the study of the political economy.

Du Bois excelled under the guidance of Schmoller, for whose research seminar he created a study that compared sharecropping in America with peasant proprietorship in Germany. Schmoller maintained that the roots of social policy and eventual social reform were to be discovered in the careful, deliberate collection of comparative scientific facts. Scholars were to remain detached collecting data, addressing what *is* rather than being preoccupied with what ought to be. According to Schmoller, recommendations and social reform would be based on available findings.

The work Du Bois created under Schmoller evolved into a larger economic analysis of large and small agricultural systems in the southern United States. This research and written work was judged strong enough to gain a doctorate from the university, but despite the support of his professors he was not awarded the degree. The university had a policy that students needed to attend the school for three years to complete graduate work, and since Du Bois could only afford two, and the Slater Fund was unwilling to support even one more semester at Berlin, he was forced to return to the United States to be confirmed with a doctorate from Harvard.

Even though the young Du Bois did not receive a German doctorate, he cherished the educational growth he experienced at Berlin. He also relished the respite from American racism. "From the physical provincialism of America and the psychological provincialism of my rather narrow race problem into which I was born and which seemed to me the essence of life," he later reflected, "I was transplanted and startled into a realization of the real centers of modern civilization and into at least a momentary escape from my own social problems." In addition, unlike his time in Nashville or Cambridge, he interacted with the local white communities. He had expected to find the same racial prejudices that he experienced in America, but to his delight he did not. During his time abroad he dated German and Dutch women and passed the time with his fellow students. He also took part in the larger society, attending political events and speaking to Germans at common social and drinking establishments throughout the city and country. The impact on his worldview was profound. "I became more human: learned the place in life of 'Wine, Women, and Song,'" he wrote, and he "ceased to hate people simply because they belonged to one race or color."

In late spring of 1893 Du Bois began to travel the continent, going as far as his limited funds would allow. He traveled to, among other locations, Switzerland, Hungary, and Austria, where he observed discrimination against various minorities. Throughout his explorations he was often mistaken for a Gypsy or a Jew, which gave him a distinct advantage to understanding European society. Studying how discrimination affected the lives of these groups, particularly the lives of Jews in Europe, allowed him to recognize similarities to the plight of African Americans back in the United States. He also traveled to Venice and went down as far south as the Mediterranean city of Naples, where he witnessed a type of regional discrimination that led some to proclaim, "Africa starts south of Rome."

Du Bois's European travels, particularly his German experience, were tremendously impactful on his life and outlook. On his twenty-fifth birthday he privately celebrated with a little ceremony and wrote an essay in which he assessed his current condition and his future. "I am striving to make my life all that life may be—and I am limiting that strife only in so far as that strife is incompatible with others of my brothers and sisters making their lives similar. The crucial question now is," he noted, "where that limit comes. I am too often puzzled to know. . . . I am firmly convinced that my own best development is not one and the same with the best development of the world and here I am willing to sacrifice. That sacrifice to the world's good becomes too soon sickly sentimentality. I therefore take the world that the Unknown lay in my hands and work for the rise of the Negro people, taking for granted that their best development means the best development of the world." He concluded, "These are my plans: to make a name in science, to make a name in literature and thus to raise my race. Or perhaps to raise the visible empire in Africa thro' England, France, or Germany. I wonder what will be the outcome? Who knows?"

More directly, as he explained to the trustees of the Slater Fund, "My plan is something like this: to get a position in one of the Negro universities, and to seek to build up there a department of history and social science, with two objects in view: (a) to study scientifically the Negro question past and present with a view to its best solution, and (b) to collect capable young Negro students, and to see how far they are capable of furthering, by independent study and research, the best scientific work of the day."

Du Bois was an ambitious twenty-five-year-old, and he never deviated from his commitment to help his people through research, education, and activism over the next seventy years. When he completed his studies and returned to America in the summer of 1894, Du Bois was the most highly educated black man in American history. He was the perfect repudiation of white America's pronouncements of black inferiority. But as he looked at his traveling companions, European immigrants from Russia, England, Poland, Germany, France, Greece, and Austria, he was cognzant that once they reached America, began to learn the language, and lost or suppressed their ethnic distinction, they "might easily have a better chance for life than I in my own country."

Du Bois later recalled remembering a little French girl's response as all the passengers' eyes caught a glimpse of the Statue of Liberty in New York harbor. "I know not what multitude of emotions surged through others," he recalled, but he remembered "that mischievous little French girl whose eyes twinkled as she said: 'Oh yes the Statue of Liberty! With its back toward America, and its face toward France!'"

Chapter Two

The Study of the Negro

I knew . . . that practically my sole chance of earning of living combined with study was to teach, and after my work . . . in United States history, I conceived the idea of applying philosophy to an historical interpretation of race relations.
—W. E. B. Du Bois, 1968

The Fisk-, Harvard-, and German-educated, twenty-seven-year-old Du Bois returned to America in search of a job. In the near-decade he had spent gaining a postsecondary education, the southern states, backed by violence, intimidation, and the invocation of white supremacist racial politics, continued to pass legislation stripping African American citizens of their civil, social, and political rights. At the same time black citizens' rights in the North were also being increasingly curbed, with the active collusion of the federal government. In a series of rulings the Supreme Court first gave impetus to the legalizing of segregation in public accommodations by invalidating the Civil Rights Act of 1875 a short eight years after its passage in *United States v. Stanley*, commonly known as the Civil Rights Cases. Then, in 1896, as Du Bois returned to America, the court confirmed its 1883 ruling with its famous *Plessy v. Ferguson* decision, which legalized segregation on railway cars as long as the accommodations were separate but equal. The slow, methodical creation of a system of de jure and de facto segregation now known as Jim Crow was accompanied by a reign of terror against black individuals and the community. As historian Edward Ayers noted, unprosecuted white lawlessness and the "violence of lynching was a way for white people to reconcile weak governments with a demand for an impossibly high level of racial mastery, a way of terrorizing blacks into acquiescence."

This is the climate to which Du Bois returned, or as he later recalled, upon arrival in New York he was "suddenly dropped back into 'nigger'-hating America!" Furthermore, it is in this atmosphere that the most educated African American began to build his career as an academic. Confined by the racism of the time, he began searching for a teaching position at black colleges throughout the country. Although he had no training to teach languages, he accepted a position as chair of classics and professor of Latin and Greek at Wilberforce University. He took the appointment after finding no opening at Howard, Hampton, or Fisk and before he received offers to teach at Lincoln Institute in Missouri and Tuskegee Institute in Alabama.

Wilberforce was created in 1856 by a group of white Methodists but became the first college owned and operated by African Americans when the African Methodist Episcopal Church, under the guidance of Bishop Daniel Alexander Payne, purchased it in 1863. To Du Bois the black-led school seemed at first an ideal location to conduct his research and educate the leadership class of the community. However, Du Bois "landed" in Xenia, Ohio, "with the cane and glove of [his] German student days, with [his] rather inflated ideas of what a 'university' ought to be." To state it bluntly, he stuck out in the town and at the university. He found himself "against a stone wall. Nothing stirred," he explained, "before my impatient pounding! Or if it stirred, it soon slept again." Unhappy and unable to fully begin his research, strapped by the financially deficient university and the intellectually stifling work of teaching Greek, Latin, English, and German, Du Bois quickly began to look for an exit.

Additionally, though he did his best to avoid it, the religious fervor of the school proved to be too much for the young professor. He kept to himself in his room conducting his studies but was often interrupted by the services. He once wrote in his diary that he was "driven almost to distraction by the wild screams, cries, groans, and shrieks" rumbling from inside the chapel. He refused to take part in the religious revivals because they interrupted class time, and Du Bois also caused quite a stir when he rejected a request to lead a class in prayer. As he remembered years later, "It took a great deal of explaining to the board of bishops why a professor in Wilberforce should not be able at all times and sundry to address God in extemporaneous prayer."

Du Bois's aversion to the intrusion of religion on his studies and his work in training the leadership of the race should not be taken as a rejection of faith. In fact, while at Wilberforce, he confessed in the pages of his diary that he was "a Christian," and throughout life he infused his writing with religious imagery and acknowledgment of faith. But as he tried to explain to the American Methodist Episcopal (AME) bishops at Wilberforce, he was raised in the Congregational Church in northwestern Massachusetts, where "the ordinary layman doesn't lead in prayer. He sits and listens and that sort of thing, but . . . he doesn't take active part in any religious exercises." In the end he was comfortable in his own faith and throughout his life would express it in his own manner.

Despite finding a way to exist on campus among the religious zeal, Du Bois believed that his days were numbered at the school. The seriousness of the fellow professors and student body was not up to his standards. He protested when powerful AME Bishop Benjamin W. Arnett proposed an appointment for his son, whom Du Bois believed was inadequately trained. The combination of these factors led him to write Booker T. Washington in early 1896 to let him know he was looking to relocate. Then, almost by fate, in the fall of the same year, Du Bois received an offer from the University of Pennsylvania to study the black community of Philadelphia.

With eagerness, the frustrated Du Bois accepted the offer, but before leaving Ohio for the City of Brotherly Love, at the age of twenty-eight, Du Bois married Nina Gomer, a "slender, quiet and dark-eyed" student from Cedar Rapids, Iowa. Despite his frequent affairs, the two would be married for fifty-four years, until her death in 1950, and while apart for long stretches at a time, both tirelessly supported his work for the race. He later stated, however, that "she must often have been lonesome and wanted more regular and personal companionship." "Poor Nina," he proclaimed after her passing, "I should never have left her so much."

In addition to his nuptials he saw the publication of his first monograph, his dissertation, *The Suppression of the African Slave-Trade to the United States of America, 1638-1870*, as the first volume of the Harvard Historical Studies. The work traces the growth of legislation and enforcement against the transatlantic slave trade from the colonial period until after the American Civil War. In the book, Du Bois concludes that the abolition of the trade failed abysmally because of spotty enforcement and apathy on the part of the government and the white public. Moreover, he considered America's ban on the trade a "dead letter" and estimated that the illegal trade brought "not less than 250,000" Africans into America from 1808 to the Civil War. This number proved to be an overestimation on the doctor's part and remains one of the criticisms of the book today. The young scholar, however, could not have understood, or accurately calculated, the massive growth of the American slave population due to biological reproduction.

As one would expect from a scholar trained by Albert Bushnell Hart and Gustav Schmoller, *The Suppression of the African Slave-Trade* meticulously gathered and traced the voluminous legislation developed by the various colonies, as well as the efforts by the subsequent states and the U.S. Congress, to curtail the trade in Africans. The book was widely reviewed and favorably received when it was published. As the *Atlantic Monthly* stated in April 1897, "Dr. Du Bois has shown good judgment in the choice of his subject, and has been most industrious in gathering and arranging his material; for though the substance of his monograph may be reached more succinctly in Lalor's *Cyclopaedia of Political Science*, he has given a very full array of authorities for all his facts, and has furnished a workmanlike chronological conspectus of colonial, state, national, and international legislation, and a good bibliography. All this apparatus looks well, and Dr. Du Bois has laid students under obligation to him." For more than fifty years *The Suppression of the African Slave-Trade* was considered a standard on the transatlantic trade, and though some of his larger interpretations have been weakened or surpassed, the book continues to serve historians who wish to find in one place the legislation used by opponents to end the barbaric practice of trading human beings across the Atlantic to North America.

Shortly after the publication of *The Suppression of the African Slave-Trade*, Du Bois and his bride of three months landed in Philadelphia, where he was to do the first sociological study of African Americans in America, amid "dirt, drunkenness, poverty, and crime." Du Bois and Nina had misgivings about moving to the city. Neither had lived in an area "where kids played intriguing games like 'cops and lady bums'; and where in the night when pistols popped, you didn't get up lest you find you couldn't." "Murder sat on our doorstep," Du Bois later explained, "police were our government, and philanthropy dropped in with periodic advice."

Du Bois's reservations and thoughts about crime, cleanliness, and the general makeup of the black community were natural for the period and proof of the need for his scientific, factual study. As he began his study of the black community of the seventh ward, the nation as a whole looked upon black crime, poverty, and lack of education as confirmation of black inferiority and by so doing justified their racism. The period was not receptive to social liberalism or even "progressivism." Social Darwinism was the prevailing social philosophy, which gave intellectual legitimacy to white supremacy. Stemming largely from the minds of those educated at white southern universities, it had gained acceptance among northern intellectuals as well, and much of this racial philosophy found a growing audience in northern journals such as *Forum, North American Review, Arena, Harper's Weekly, The Nation, Atlantic Monthly, Popular Science Monthly,* and *Outlook.* The sentiment was bolstered by the popularity of a number of larger studies such as William P. Calhoun's *The Caucasian and The Negro in the United States. They Must Separate. If Not, Then Extermination. A Proposed Solution: Colonization* (1902). In direct correlation to this rising racial ideology, segregation in public—restaurants, hotels, libraries, schools, transportation—became an established fact of life. Lynching was the common response to perceived black crime but was actually a form of social control. Between 1898 and 1900 nearly three hundred African Americans were murdered by this extralegal means throughout the country.

In response, the black community turned inward to try to transform segregation to their own advantage. As the nation adopted an ideology of white supremacy and black inferiority, African Americans countered by asserting racial solidarity, racial pride, and self-reliance. Du Bois, however, though he certainly agreed with those notions, sought a different approach. He wanted to confront white America with facts to disprove their stereotypes and generalizations. He believed scientific study and education were the means to counter the ideology of white supremacy. As he later stated, his study "revealed the Negro groups as a symptom, not a cause; as a striving, palpitating group, and not an inert, sick body of crime; as a long historic development and not a transient occurrence."

To demonstrate this belief, Nina and William Du Bois lived in a cramped apartment in Philadelphia's seventh ward for fifteen months while he researched the surrounding community. After this period of intense research he produced *The Philadelphia Negro,* a look at the plight of the African American community of the city. The general aim, according to Du Bois, demonstrating the continued influence of his German mentor Schmoller, was "to present the results of an inquiry . . . into the condition of the four thousand or more people of Negro blood now living in the city of Philadelphia. This inquiry . . . sought to ascertain something of the geographical distribution of this race, their occupations, and, above all, their relation to their million white fellow-citizens. The final design of the work was to lay before the public such a body of information as may be a safe guide for all efforts toward the solution of the many Negro problems of a great American city."

The final point was extremely important to Du Bois. At this stage in his career he believed that the race problem was essentially one of ignorance. He was determined to shed as much knowledge as he could, thereby providing a cure for color prejudice. "The sole aim of any society," he said, "is to settle its problems in accordance with its highest ideals, and the only rational method of accomplishing this is to study those problems in the light of the best scientific research."

The Philadelphia Negro opens with a detailed historical analysis of the city's black community. As Du Bois explained in 1897, "One can not study the Negro in freedom and come to general conclusions about his destiny without knowing his history in slavery." Combined with this historical sociology, Du Bois presented exhaustive data on the character and social institutions of the community, including statistics on health, marital and family relations, crime, education, vocational status, and literacy. In the end Du Bois believed that the study was "as complete a scientific study and answer as could have been given, with defective facts and statistics, one lone worker and little money." It is, as historian Manning Marable stated, a "powerful sociological and moral argument against institutional racism."

Some of the young scholar's New England, Calvinist, moral ethics were revealed in his criticisms of the black community in the pages of *The Philadelphia Negro*. Du Bois deplored the vice and "sexual looseness" that was "the prevailing sin of the mass of the Negro population." He also criticized the criminal element of the community, noting with some dismay: "it is not well to clean a cesspool until one know where the refuse can be disposed of without general harm." He charged the church with failing to combat social corruption and moral decay and censured parents for not reinforcing the value of formal education.

Du Bois demonstrated his Calvinist upbringing and a strong support of the politics of respectability and progressive reform with his comments about the home and work ethic of the community.

> Efforts to stop . . . crime must commence in the Negro homes; they must cease to be, as they often are, breeders of idleness and extravagance and complaint. Work, continuous and intensive; work, although be it menial and poorly rewarded; work, though done in travail of soul and sweat of brow, must be so impressed upon Negro children as the road to salvation, that a child would feel it a greater disgrace to be idle than to do the humblest labor. The homely virtues of honesty, truth, and chastity, must be installed in the cradle, and although it is hard to teach self-respect to a people whose million fellow-

citizens half-despise them, yet it must be taught as the surest road to gain the respect of others.

Despite his heavy-handed criticism of the black community, Du Bois did demonstrate the importance of environmentalism in the plight of the black community and in so doing began an attack on the racist idea that racial inequalities were natural, inevitable, and inborn. He showed that many of his critiques and at least some of the traits assigned to blacks—criminality, laziness, and sexual promiscuity—were false or a result of social influence, and therefore he argued that they could and should be changed.

In the end Du Bois walked away from the seventh ward with new ideas and assumptions. As he stated in the spring of 1897, "I became painfully aware that merely being born in a group, does not necessarily make one possessed of complete knowledge concerning it. I had learned far more from the Philadelphia Negroes than I had taught them concerning the Negro Problem."

While the young scholar's life program was outlined more clearly at the end of his research in Philadelphia, he was out of a job, frustrated that Penn did not offer him temporary instructorship at the college or at the Wharton School. "White [Harvard] classmates of lower academic rank" than he had become "full professors at Pennsylvania and Chicago," he noted with consternation. What bothered him was that neither fellow scholars nor the school ever entertained the idea of retaining him. As he explained, "I know an insult when I see it."

Looking back, the insult was a clear indication of American racism. By the end of the nineteenth century Du Bois had emerged as one of the most formidable American intellectuals and scholars of any race. As the holder of a Harvard doctorate and the author of two well-received research monographs, he should have been a viable candidate for a position at one of America's leading universities. But in 1898, though he was trained by some of the leading scholars in the United States and Germany and despite the fact that his research was respected and well received, no white university would have ever considered hiring an African American for a permanent professorship. Thankfully, historically black Atlanta University, a school founded in 1865 by the American Missionary Association and the oldest American graduate institution that serves a predominantly black student body, extended him an offer, and he accepted.

Du Bois, at first the only African American on faculty, was hired to teach economics and history and direct the Sociological Laboratory and the Atlanta University Conferences. The year before, George Bradford, a trustee, had suggested that Atlanta initiate a series of annual conferences to study the effect of urban problems on African Americans. Hampton and Tuskegee institutes had already begun studies of rural black communities and held annual conferences to disseminate the research and information. Atlanta wanted to situate themselves as the leading institution researching the condition of the black community, and they sought to hire the foremost scholar in the field.

Du Bois taught five or six classes each year, but with his European goatee and proper manners, students viewed the dapper young professor as demanding and somewhat aloof. He gave long reading assignments, was always impeccably dressed, and would often walk past students without acknowledging them. The students did, however, see a different man when he played

Figure 2.1.   W. E. B. Du Bois with colleagues at Atlanta University. Courtesy University of Massachusetts Archives.

tennis or when he displayed anything other than the "formal dignity we knew indoors."

Over time he won the students over and they warmed up to his teaching. Some of his classes became the most popular on campus, and when it was his turn to lecture at the weekly prayer meeting, the attendance overflowed. The small seminars held at his residence were especially well liked. Students recalled that these select experiences were delightful with an intimate atmosphere. In this setting he made students feel special. Du Bois seemed more comfortable, exchanging his suit for a smoking jacket, and was a "charming host . . . thoughtful and entertaining. He told anecdotes and showed that he did understand his students . . . he seemed very relaxed in his apartment, very witty and permissive." The material was often discussed over cookies, coffee, and special cigarettes imported from around the world.

In addition to teaching, Du Bois continued the work he started with *The Philadelphia Negro*. Both the young professor and the leaders of the school believed that the university was ideally located to facilitate research of the black community. The university, Du Bois explained, was "situated within a few miles of the geographical centre of the Negro population of the nation, and is, therefore, near the centre of that congeries of human problems which cluster round the Black American." In his research and the Atlanta conferences the doctor chose not to focus on social reform but rather to work toward "the collection of a basic body of fact concerning the social condition to exact measurement whenever or wherever occasion permitted."

To accomplish such an agenda, he first "laid down an ambitious plan for a hundred years of study," through which he "hoped to make the laws of social living clearer, surer and more definite." Because of financial limitations, unavailability of suitable data, and lack of tested methods of investigation, he was forced to alter the program. The studies, however, accomplished a tremendous amount. *"The Atlanta University Publications*, consisting of 18 monographs published between 1896 and 1914, were the first attempts to study scientifically the problems of the American Negro anywhere in the world; the first studies to make factual, empirical evidence the center of sociological work on the Negro." As in *The Philadelphia Negro*, through these studies Du Bois assaulted the prejudiced generalizations made by whites.

During his time at Atlanta University, the studies and Du Bois's research in general received inadequate funding. As he sarcastically commented in a remark many academics would tweak, but endorse today:

We can go to the South Sea Islands half way around the world and beat and
shoot weak people longing for freedom into the slavery of American colored
prejudice at the cost of hundreds of millions, and yet at Atlanta University we
beg annually and beg in vain for the paltry sum of $500 simply to aid us in
replacing gross and vindictive ignorance of race conditions with enlightening
knowledge and systematic observation.

Despite the financial problems, and with the help of limited outside funding, Du Bois managed to continue the program. Although it is difficult to
assess the impact of the Atlanta Studies, it can safely be said that they formed
an impressive body of research, which served to strengthen racial pride
among a large segment of the black community. The most significant effect
of the studies was to destroy some of the many myths that had arisen about
blacks by gathering empirical data. Biographer Elliott Rudwick claimed that
the studies provided blacks with appropriate arguments against their low
status in society, which arguments carried the imprimatur of social science.

Some of the volumes have not stood the test of time, but others, such as
The College-Bred Negro (1900, 1910) and *The Negro Common School*
(1901, 1911), hold excellent data for today's scholars and give a glimpse into
the black school system at the turn of the nineteenth century. Another strong
set of studies within the collection, according to Rudwick, is *The Negro
Artisan* (1902, 1912). Through a collection of questionnaires Du Bois was
able to provide information on, among others things, which unions admitted
black workers, payment comparisons between black and white workers, and
the course material of industrial and training schools and its relevance to the
workplace. Moreover, once the second volume was released in 1912, com-
parison data was used to estimate whether black workers were holding their
own in the various trades.

The strong research and analysis and the overall importance of the Atlanta Studies were recognized quickly. When the first volume was released in
1902, *Outlook* published a review that stated: "no student of the race problem, no person who would either think or speak upon it intelligently, can
afford to be ignorant of the facts brought out in the Atlanta series of sociological studies of the conditions and the progress of the negro. . . . The hand of
the skilled and thorough investigator is conspicuous throughout."

This was the general opinion of the work Du Bois and his conferences
were producing in Atlanta under difficult financial conditions. "The work
done under the direction of the Atlanta Conference is entitled to the respect-
ful and thoughtful consideration of every man interested in any aspect of the

life of the American Negro," remarked a reviewer in the Southern History Association Publications in 1904. "The guiding spirit of his work," he continued, "is Dr. Du Bois, and he is entitled to the utmost credit for what has been accomplished in the face of many obstacles confronting his undertaking." Such positive commentary from anyone allied with the Southern History Association at the turn of the century was a significant accomplishment for Du Bois and his work, given the organization's conservative bias at the time.

From investigating such varied subjects as Africa; education; crime; family life; the black businessman, artisan, farmer, and college student; social betterment; and health among the nation's black population, Du Bois produced a systematic "introduction into the field of race relations when other men were speculating." The studies countered generalizations and mythology. For instance, continuing the work of feminist, journalist, and anti-lynching activist Ida B. Wells-Barnett, among others, the research and analysis in some of the volumes challenged the argument that African Americans were being lynched because of accusations of rape or attempted rape. Through his work Du Bois also demonstrated that southern black children were receiving an inferior education, based on school appropriations, teacher salaries, facilities, and length of school terms, all foundational blocks of the future NAACP's arguments on the road to the *Brown v. Board of Education* (1954) decision. Furthermore, he challenged the notion that the continent of Africa had no historical past or, worse, was a vast cultural cipher.

Among the scientific research, Du Bois did make suggestions for social reform, the style of leadership the community needed, and other ideas. Overall, in the studies one sees Du Bois with a comparatively conservative program, adopting the "politics of respectability" to resist and explain away the negative stigmas and caricatures about African American morality. Du Bois, like others at the time, claimed respectability through manners and morality. An avenue flourished for African Americans to assert the will and agency to redefine themselves outside the prevailing racist discourse. Self-help, duty and discipline, efficiency, thrift, intraracial economic cooperation, group pride, the responsibility of the black "aristocracy" to encourage and assist in the elevation of the black masses—these were among Du Bois's charges to African Americans. The time at Atlanta and with the studies, however, was the beginning of his real life. They were years of great spiritual upturning, of the making and unmaking of ideals, of hard work and hard play.

Here I found myself. I lost most of my mannerisms, I grew more broadly
human, made my closest and most holy friendships, and studied human beings.
I became widely acquainted with the conditions of my people. I realized the
terrific odds which faced them.

Through the Atlanta conferences and studies, Du Bois established a national reputation as the leading social scientist of black America. The fea-
tured speaker at the 1902 conference, Booker T. Washington, principal of
Tuskegee Institute in Alabama, observed that he had a "keen interest and
appreciation" for the doctor's research and predicted that his efforts "will
stand for years as a monument to his ability, wisdom and faithfulness."
While Du Bois may never have been fully satisfied with the studies, lack of
financial support to adequately fund the research was the main frustration.
The Atlanta conferences and their subsequent publications had a tremendous
impact and lasting legacy. These sociological studies on black life and culture stood, with a few other works, against the flood of nonscientific and
racist dogma—which included Charles Carroll's *The Negro a Beast: Or In
the Image of God* (1900); Thomas Dixon's *The Leopard's Spots* (1902);
Robert W. Shufeldt's *The Negro, A Menace to American Civilization* (1907);
and William Graham Sumner's *Folkways* (1907). At a period when white
social scientists and novelists denied the humanity of African Americans, Du
Bois established their social diversity and integrity.

In addition to the Atlanta Studies, in many ways to bolster the impact of
his work on the mind of the educated American citizen, Du Bois wrote most
of his sociological pieces during this period, with many published in mainstream white magazines and journals. Among other articles, he published
"The Negroes of Farmville, Virginia: A Social Study" (1898); "The Study of
the Negro Problem" (1898); "The Negro in the Black Belt" (1899); "The
Negro and Crime" (1899); "The Negro Landholders of Georgia" (1901);
"Sociology Hesitant" (1904); "Race Friction between Black and White"
(1908); and "The Economic Aspects of Race Prejudice" (1910). Furthermore, during this period in Atlanta Du Bois sought to make a greater impact
in the black community by producing two popular magazines. First, he
founded *The Moon Illustrated Weekly* (1906–1907), the first of five publications he would create over his lifetime. Through the pages of *The Moon* he
sought to interpret "a new race consciousness to the world and [to reveal] the
inner meaning of the modern world to the merging races." Each issue of the
weekly contained national and international coverage, many of the pieces

written by Du Bois himself, and reprinted a broad range of editorials on civil rights and labor topics drawn from papers throughout the country.

After the collapse of *The Moon* in 1907, he initiated another publication along with two friends, Freeman Murray and Lafayette Hershaw. *The Horizon: A Journal of the Color Line* was somewhat more successful, lasting until 1910. According to biographer David Levering Lewis, *The Horizon* was a "dress rehearsal for a career in propaganda journalism. Its words were like darts, sharper than *The Moon*'s barbs had been, and the targets were larger." Like its predecessor *The Horizon* attempted to cover domestic and international issues and developments. Du Bois and Hershaw paid increasing attention to issues related to the darker peoples of the world, particularly developments in Africa and Asia. Their focus also sharpened on the growing leadership class of the community, in particular the activities of Booker T. Washington, civil rights, socialism, and the Republican Party.

In addition to these academic and journalistic efforts, during this period Du Bois became involved in organizational endeavors that sought to uplift the race. In the late nineteenth and early twentieth centuries African Americans created a number of associations for social uplift and solidarity as well as proposals for organization, knowledge, and protest. Throughout this era African American professionals organized the Negro Press Association, the Afro-American League, the National Association of Colored Women's Clubs, and the National Negro Business League, to name a few. This professional organizing spilled over into culture, as communities organized literary and historical organizations such as the Bethel Literary Historical Association in Washington, D.C.; the Brooklyn Literary Union in New York; and the American Negro Historical Society of Philadelphia. These groups, according to historian Manning Marable, "stimulated a growing identification with Africa's cultural heritage, while providing an ideological justification for race-conscious, separatist organizations in American political and economic life."

While Du Bois was finishing *The Philadelphia Negro*, a group of African American intellectuals formed a national educational society that sought to promote science, art, literature, and higher education; publish scholarly works; and defend the black population from vicious attacks. This group, the American Negro Academy, held its first formal meeting in Washington, D.C., on March 5, 1897, and boasted some of the most prominent intellectuals and educators as its original members: newspaper publisher and Howard law school graduate John Wesley Cromwell; Presbyterian minister Francis James Grimké; Howard University professor Kelly Miller; Episcopalian min-

ister and pan-Africanist Alexander Crummell; Wilberforce University professors William S. Scarborough and Edward E. Clarke; and Du Bois. During
its twenty-seven-year existence the academy published twenty-two "occasional papers" on topics ranging from civil and political rights, religion, and
history to black institutions and their place in American society.

In the evening proceedings of the academy's inaugural meeting, Du Bois
presented a paper, "The Conservation of the Races." In the piece he argued
that the world's great races had distinct cultural and "spiritual" characteris-
tics, and some of the racial groups, such as Africans, had only begun to give
"to civilization the full spiritual message which they are capable of giving."
The great African American intellectuals, presumably led by members of the
academy, needed to rise up and begin to write the future, as well as reveal the
unique past of the world's racial groups. Du Bois declared that they must
promote the "development of Negro genius, of Negro literature and art, of
Negro spirit, only Negroes bound and weld together. . . ." "Negroes inspired
by one vast ideal," he argued, "can work out in its fullness the great message
we have for humanity."

Long before the terms *cultural pluralism* or *transnationalism* were in use,
Du Bois was calling for the world to see the uniqueness of racial groups
spiritually and culturally, not biologically, and to embrace those differences.
He asked:

> What after all, am I? Am I an American or am I a Negro? Can I be both? Or is
> it my duty to cease to be a Negro as soon as possible and be an American? If I
> strive as a Negro, am I not perpetuating the very cleft that threatens and
> separates black and white America? Does my black blood place upon me any
> more obligation to assert my nationality than German, or Irish or Italian blood
> would?

Du Bois offered his own resolution to the "riddle that puzzles so many of
us":

> We are Americans, not only by birth and citizenship, but by our political
> ideals, our language, our religion. Farther than that, our Americanism does not
> go. At that point, we are Negroes, members of a vast historic race that from the
> very dawn of creation has slept, but half awakening in the dark forests of its
> African fatherland. We are the first fruits of this new nation, the harbinger of
> the black to-morrow which is destined to soften the whiteness of the Teutonic
> to-day. We are that people whose subtle sense of song has given America its
> only American music, its only American fairy tales, its only touch of pathos

and humor amid its mad money-getting plutocracy. As such, it is our duty to conserve our physical powers, our intellectual endowments, our spiritual ideals; as a race we must strive by race organization, by race solidarity . . . to the realization of that broader humanity which freely recognizes differences in men, but sternly deprecates inequality in their opportunities of development.

Du Bois's address was greeted with "prolonged applause." There was some discussion, but overall the address was heralded as a great success and was published within the year as a fifteen-page pamphlet to be circulated as one of the weapons in the educational war against the rising tide of white supremacy. It was also one of his early successes as a young scholar. As biographer David Levering Lewis argued, "The Conservation of the Races" "lobbed some of the most powerful projectiles of racial and cultural exclusivism onto the ideological landscape of the twentieth century; their repercussions as black nationalism, black Zionism, Pan-Africanism, black aestheticism, and isms yet to discharge in the next century, have caused regimes to shudder and crumble and very probably will shake future ones to their foundations."

The protocultural nationalism that appeared in "The Conservation of the Races" would reappear throughout Du Bois's life, at times stronger than others, but often present. It was certainly present in the summer of 1900. Du Bois traveled across the Atlantic to participate in a conference that sought to organize Africans throughout the Diaspora on issues of common concern. The Pan-African Conference had been organized by Trinidadian barrister Henry Sylvester Williams, who had moved to London and organized a Pan-African Association, whose goals were "to secure the African throughout the world true civil and political rights" and "to ameliorate the conditions of our brothers on the continent of Africa, America and other parts of the world."

From July 23 to 25, Du Bois and about thirty other West Indians and African Americans met at Westminster Town Hall to organize around the principles of the association. The delegates drafted "An Address to the Nations of the World," which called for democratic treatment of Africans throughout the Diaspora and for the end of colonization of the continent of Africa. During his address, "To the Nations of the World," Du Bois delivered one of his most famous lines and proclamations: "the problem of the twentieth century is the color line, the question as to how far differences of race, which show themselves chiefly in the color of the skin and the texture of the hair, are going to be made, hereafter, the basis of denying to over half the world the right of sharing to their utmost ability the opportunities and privileges of modern civilization." Additionally, Du Bois, echoing his American Negro Academy address, called for Africans throughout the world to "take courage, strive ceaselessly, and fight bravely, [so that] they may prove to the world their incontestable right to be counted among the great brotherhood of mankind."

While the attendees were enthusiastic, the results of the first Pan-African Conference were minimal. Nearly fifty years later in his *The World and Africa* (1947), Du Bois remarked, "This meeting had no deep roots in Africa itself, and the movement and the idea died for a generation." Williams returned to the Caribbean to organize associations throughout the islands, and while Du Bois's and others' interests in Africa continued to rise, their Diasporic organizational efforts would slow for a couple of decades.

Despite the limited success of the Pan-African Conference, Du Bois's career had taken off since he and his family moved to Atlanta. Yet in personal, private, domestic, everyday life, these years of southern living were difficult for the Du Bois family. In 1898, the new Atlanta residents lost their eighteen-month-old son, Burghardt Gomer Du Bois, after he fell ill because of exposure to sewage pollution in the city's water system. "Blithe was the

Figure 2.2.   Family portrait of Du Bois, his wife, Nina, and their baby son, Burghardt. Courtesy University of Massachusetts Archives.

morning of his burial, with bird and song and sweet-smelling flowers," Du Bois recalled.

> The trees whispered to the grass, but the children sat with hushed faces. And yet it seemed a ghostly unreal day—the wraith of life. We seemed to rumble down an unknown street behind a little white bundle of posies, with the shadow of a song in our ears. The busy city dinned about us; they did not say much, those pale-faced hurrying men and women; they did not say much,—they only glanced and said "Niggers!"

Du Bois was in agony: "I am no coward, to shrink before a rugged rush of the storm, not even quail before the awful shadow of the Veil. But harken, O Death! Is not this life hard enough, but that thou must needs enter here,— thou, O Death?" Burghardt's death "tore our lives in two," Du Bois wrote. "I threw myself more completely into my work, while most reason for living left the soul of my wife. Another child, a girl, came later, but my wife never forgave God for the unhealable wound."

It is also during this period that his disillusionment with scholarship as a weapon grew. Living in the South as white supremacy lowered its veil on the region, indeed the whole nation, it became increasingly difficult to believe that just education could end racial oppression. Jim Crow segregation continued to surround Du Bois and encroach on his and his family's life and consciousness. Georgia passed legislation segregating all public streetcars in 1891, and by 1900 most southern states had similar codes. Between 1889 and 1899 the average number of lynchings was nearly two hundred per year nationally. Atlanta and other southern cities began to pass laws requiring Jim Crow restrictions in public accommodations. Finally, in 1905, the Separate Park Law was adopted by the Georgia legislature, restricting black citizens from public parks. Du Bois and his family limited their contact with white Atlanta and the South, but he did have to travel and research from time to time and was often confronted with extreme indignities.

The lynching of Sam Hose, a black laborer from the region, in 1899, also shook his confidence that attitudes and actions would change if only people knew the facts. After finding the knuckles of Hose "at a grocery store" he decided "one could not be a calm, cool, and detached scientist while Negroes were lynched, murdered and starved." Another event that changed his political outlook was the Atlanta Riot of 1906. For three days, white civilians and police mercilessly attacked blacks. During the violence four blacks had been murdered and scores of African Americans were terrorized, injured, and dispersed from the city. Du Bois was in Alabama when the violence began, and he rushed back to Atlanta as quickly as he could. On the train from Lowndes County to Atlanta he wrote one of his famous poems, "A Litany of Atlanta." "Listen to us," the words cried off the page. "Thy children; our faces dark with doubt, are made a mockery in Thy sanctuary. With uplifted hands we front Thy heaven, O God, crying: we beseech Thee to hear us, good Lord!" Du Bois continued, "Surely, Thou too art not white, O Lord a pale, bloodless, heartless, thing? . . . But whisper—speak—call, great God, for Thy silence is white terror to our hearts!"

Du Bois did not remain silent and unresponsive to the physical, psychological, and economic spread of white supremacy. He protested against certain occurrences taking place in Georgia and the nation. The year after he arrived in Atlanta, the Georgia legislature debated passing disfranchisement laws. Du Bois, along with several others, sent a statement of protest to the legislature. He later followed by publishing a brief article on the subject in the *Independent*, in which he expressed his support for the bill as long as the restrictions were applied equally to both races. Such a position was often taken by a number of black leaders, including T. Thomas Fortune and Booker T. Washington, as southern states systematically stripped the franchise from the African American electorate. Du Bois also became involved in challenging attempts to cut the appropriations to black schools in Georgia as well as to exclude African Americans from the new Carnegie Library in Atlanta. Finally, when the state legislature passed a law prohibiting African Americans from using the Pullman car facilities, Du Bois considered filing suit, gaining the support of Booker T. Washington in his efforts, but later decided not to move forward.

The continued impingement of Jim Crow segregation on his and his loved ones' lives, along with the increasing violence of the South, symbolized by Sam Hose and the riot of 1906, increasingly moved Du Bois to embrace a more radicalized political outlook. He continued to question whether, as he had so firmly believed before, education was the key to enlightenment and would be sufficient to end racism in America, or whether more direct measures were needed.

Chapter Three

Of Du Bois, Booker T. Washington, and Others

A Challenge of Leadership

Once they tell us, Jehovah, that in the great shadows of the past Thou hast whispered to a quivering people, saying, "Be not afraid." . . . Grant us today, O God, that fearlessness that rests on confidence in the ultimate rightness of things. Let us be afraid neither of mere physical hurt, nor of the unpopularity of our cause; let us turn toward the battle of life undismayed.

—W. E. B. Du Bois, 1910

Among the terrorization, discrimination, and government abandonment that the black communities were experiencing in the late nineteenth and early twentieth centuries, the nation as a whole was going through a major political realignment. The ideals of the Progressive Era were affecting the major political parties as leaders promoted policies designed to encourage good government, regulation of business and industry, an end to monopolies, pure food and drug reform, better wages and working conditions for laborers, improved housing, and a variety of social programs directed toward the vast numbers of immigrants flooding into America.

A journalistic, investigative spirit pushed the national sentiment of progressive reform. Muckraking journalists filled newspapers and magazines with challenges to governmental corruption, corporate malfeasance, and horrendous housing and working conditions. Upton Sinclair published his withering indictment of Chicago's slaughterhouses, *The Jungle* (1906). In addition, Jacob Riis, with his camera, made visible to the nation the living conditions of immigrants, the poor, and the homeless in New York City with the publication of *How the Other Half Lives* (1890).

This investigative muckraking style influenced the writing on race relations in the Progressive Era as well, and the desire to solve the Negro problem or reform race relations permeated the white and black press of the period. Ray Stannard Baker, following the 1906 Atlanta Riot, wrote an influential collection of essays on race relations. Baker traveled the country investigating the effects of segregation and published his findings in *McClure's* and *American Magazine*, before publishing the pieces collectively as *Following the Color Line* in 1908. Among his findings and recommendations on Jim Crow's effects on the black and white communities, Baker exposed what he saw as two distinct factions in African American intellectual thought, one headed by Booker T. Washington and the other by Du Bois. Simplistically, Baker characterized Washington's group as being southern and made up of the masses and Du Bois's pack as a collection of northern based African American intellectuals.

While Washington and Du Bois came to epitomize the split of black leadership at the turn of the twentieth century, they were not as separate as Baker argued, or scholars who have followed his lead. While Du Bois differed from Washington on many things, ideologically he was not so far from the "Wizard of Tuskegee," the most powerful black man in America. Washington, born a slave and educated at Hampton Institute in Virginia, was becoming a leading voice in the black community during the 1890s. In 1881, he became the principal of Tuskegee Normal and Industrial Institute in Alabama, an all-black school teaching self-determination, which quickly equaled other black institutions of the day. Tuskegee emphasized industrial education and economic independence in an area dominated by sharecropping. The school soon became larger than the town as Washington bought surrounding farmland and sold it at low rates to create a community of land- and home-owners. The institute and its surrounding community became the model black town, an example of Washington's vision of self-reliant communities that could turn segregation into autonomous development and economic opportunity through separation and strength in numbers.

Washington's subsequent transformation into the preeminent black leader, however, took him and his influence beyond the grounds of Tuskegee. On September 18, 1895, he gave a speech at the Cotton States and International Exposition in Atlanta, which address is now famously known as the "Atlanta

Compromise." In it, Washington contended that if left alone, blacks could prosper and contribute greatly to the nation. In an attempt to disarm southern whites, Washington declared that agitation for social equality was not where African Americans needed to put their energies, and that in "purely social" matters the races could "be as separate as the fingers, yet one as the hand in all things essential to mutual progress." In return for relinquishing the demand for immediate civil and political rights, Washington called on whites to remove any barriers to black economic advancement as the two races worked together but separately to uplift the South and the nation. After the Atlanta Exposition address and the death of Frederick Douglass earlier that year, Washington rose to become the principal negotiator between the races. Andrew Carnegie, William Baldwin, and other white philanthropists gave money to uplift the race, and Washington allocated the funds to areas that he saw fit, such as the promotion of black businesses and support of other black schools. He also became a key political advisor for many Republican politicians, including Theodore Roosevelt, who looked to Washington as his foremost confidant on race issues after his election to the presidency. Washington's public philosophy—a renunciation of rights, silence on abuses, and disparagement of higher education—that gained him his place as the leader, however, could not be sustained as white racism failed to lessen, lynching continued to rise, and Jim Crow became solidified in the decade after Washington's Atlanta address. Such action was not directly Washington's fault, but despite his secret support for challenges to segregation and occasional public vocal challenges to discrimination, for many African Americans who sought a different approach to race relations he came to symbolize the steady deterioration of black rights.

When Washington's stature as a leader in the black community was rising and Du Bois's reputation as a leading intellectual voice on the issue of race was growing, the two enjoyed amiable relations. When many in the black community were critical or cautiously optimistic about Washington and his positions, Du Bois reacted to the Tuskegee principal and his speech in a positive manner. As he explained in *Dusk of Dawn*,

> When many colored papers condemned the proposition of compromise with the South, which Washington proposed, I wrote to the *New York Age* suggesting that here might be the basis of a real settlement between whites and blacks in the South, if the South opened to the Negroes the doors of economic opportunity and the Negroes cooperated with the white South in political sympathy.

Moreover, the two had congenial relations into the turn of the century. In 1899 Washington offered Du Bois a job at Tuskegee after being encouraged a couple of times by Albert Bushnell Hart to find a position for his former student. He tried his best to woo Du Bois, offering a home, a 14 percent salary increase, one course per year, and the promise that the remainder of the time would be free for research, writing, and speaking.

Du Bois decided against moving to Alabama. He may have feared, as his wife had, that he would simply "sink to the level of a ghostwriter." More than anything, however, he and his family hoped to move out of the South, not deeper into the lion's mouth of racial apartheid. Nina particularly struggled in Georgia; as David Levering Lewis has stated, "Nothing in provincial Iowa or backward Wilberforce had prepared her for the stinging apartheid in the capital of the so-called New South."

The Du Boises' struggle to negotiate life in the South became more difficult after their son's death in May 1898. The family buried the young Burghardt in Great Barrington, in the relative safety of the North. Dr. Du Bois also began to look for employment outside the former Confederacy. As he explained to Washington when he declined his offer to come to Tuskegee, he might do more for "both your & the general cause of the Negro" in the nation's capital. Thus, he asked for Washington's support to be named the superintendent of the black schools of the District of Columbia, claiming that his sponsorship "would go further probably than anyone else's."

Washington agreed, but later withdrew his support when he learned that many of his allies backed the appointment of Robert H. Terrell, a Harvard graduate who was the principal of M Street High School and husband of Mary Church Terrell. Upon this discovery Washington asked Du Bois to not use his letter of endorsement, stating instead that he had already "recommended [Du Bois] as strongly" as he could in personal conversations.

Du Bois was undoubtedly confused and unquestionably disappointed when the board of education selected Dartmouth graduate and Capital Savings Bank officer Winfield Montgomery for the position. But the disappointment did not sour the relationship between the two educators. At the turn of the century, Washington held too much influence for Du Bois to completely cut him off in 1900. In the summer of 1901, Washington invited Du Bois to be a guest at his summer place in West Virginia to relax and fish. In 1902, Du Bois invited Washington to a conference on the Negro artisan, a symposium conducted under the Atlanta University studies program. Du Bois would also teach a short session at Tuskegee the following year and would dine with Washington at his estate, The Oaks.

The control exercised by Washington and his Tuskegee Machine, as it was called by his critics because they argued that Washington and his network operated as a political network, caused the conflict between Washington and many of his contemporaries. "Contrary to most opinion," Du Bois elucidated in 1940, "the controversy as it developed was not entirely against Mr. Washington's ideas, but became the insistence upon the right of other Negroes to have and express their ideas. Things came to such a pass," he explained, "that when any Negro complained or advocated a course of action, he was silenced with the remark that Mr. Washington did not agree with this."

Du Bois always held that the two individuals could work together. As he stated in *Dusk of Dawn*, "I recognized the importance of the Negro gaining a foothold in trades and his encouragement in industry and common labor. Mr. Washington was not absolutely opposed to college training, and sent his own children to college. But he did minimize its importance, and discouraged the philanthropic support of higher education; while I openly and repeatedly criticized what seemed to me the poor work and small accomplishment of the Negro industrial school."

The two intellectuals drew inspiration for their varying beliefs from two opposing New England models. Du Bois was attracted to the educational philosophy of the New England school system, the apex being his alma mater, Harvard. Washington, on the other hand, looked to another model: one symbolized by the business-minded craftiness of the northern capitalists. Du Bois, however, would soon note that Washington's position evoked a triple paradox. First, Washington wished to make the mass of black folk property owners but publicly downplayed the need for rights, without which property could not be utilized or protected. Second, Washington advocated the development of black self-respect through augmentation of skills, but his advice that black folk submit to injustice undermined self-respect by such means. Third, the Wizard's advocacy of common and industrial schooling while depreciating higher education contradicted the reality that blacks who taught in the common and industrial schools would have to receive their own training at institutions of higher learning.

During the first few years of the century Du Bois's racial philosophy had been in transition. In this period he emphasized the importance of higher education and development of a black "Talented Tenth," as well as the need to defend and reclaim black voting rights. Most black leaders of the period agreed with the ideology of self-help and racial solidarity and on the need for economic and moral development, and Du Bois was no different. The difference for the Atlanta and Tuskegee advocates was in degree, not in kind. Whereas Washington sought to focus on the masses, Du Bois, expanding on the idea of his Atlanta neighbor Henry Morehouse, founder of Morehouse College, advocated training the "Talented Tenth" who would "be leaders of thought and missionaries of culture among their people." As he explained, "The Negro race, like all other races, is going to be saved by its exceptional men." He argued for "higher education of the Talented Tenth, who through their knowledge of modern culture could guide the American Negro into higher civilization." "I knew," he later stated, "white leadership, and that such leadership could not always be trusted to guide this group into self-realization and to its highest cultural possibilities."

Washington emphasized that the African American population should become producers and consumers, gaining an economic foundation and creating space in the workforce. They would bring recognition and respect to the community by accumulating wealth, occupation, and material acquisitions. Du Bois strove for something different. "It would not do to concentrate," he argued, "all the effort on economic well-being and forget freedom and manhood and equality. Rather Negroes must live and eat and strive, and still hold unfaltering commerce with the stars."

Therefore, even though the two individuals' ideals and approaches had significant harmonies, a wedge gradually drove them apart regarding the immediate importance of the ballot and the relative emphasis placed on industrial and higher education. While the split was festering, however, others in the community took a more critical position against the Wizard of Tuskegee, notably Ida B. Wells-Barnett. Ferdinand Barnett and his wife, Ida B. Wells-Barnett, used their Chicago newspaper, *The Conservator*, as a vehicle to attack Tuskegee. Other journalists and activists also began picking up the pen and stepping up to the lectern to criticize Washington and what they saw as his willingness to capitulate to white racism, abandon politics, and emphasize industrial education at the expense of higher education. These critics included, among others, Harry C. Smith of the Cleveland *Gazette*, John Hope, president of Atlanta Baptist College, and most notably, William Monroe Trotter, a contemporary of Du Bois's at Harvard.

Trotter, born in 1872 and the son of James Trotter, was the first African American elected to the Phi Beta Kappa honor society at Harvard College.

After college he became a successful insurance and mortgage agent. He also married a mutual friend of his and Du Bois's from the Boston area, Geraldine Pindell. Despite his successful business ventures, Trotter, unlike Washington, did not see business and the accumulation of wealth as the path for recognition and racial harmony. "[P]ursuit of business, money, civil or literary position was like building a house upon the sands, if race prejudice and persecution and public discrimination for mere color was to spread up from the South." He believed Booker T. Washington needed to be more forceful on racial injustice. He did not want to "wait until I knew the white people of the South were in that frame of mind where they were willing to listen to what I had to say," he proclaimed.

In 1901, Trotter and a friend, George W. Forbes, began publishing *The Guardian*, a newspaper dedicated to challenging Washington's leadership. From the pages of *The Guardian* Trotter asked Washington:

> To what end will your vaulting ambition hurl itself? Does not the fear of future hate and execration, does not the sacred rights and hopes of a suffering race, in no wise move you? The colored people see and understand you; they know that you have marked their very freedom for destruction, and yet, they endure you almost without murmur! O times, O evil day, upon which we have fallen!

Despite Trotter's conviction, taken collectively, he and the other opponents of Booker T. Washington were a small minority of the black community generally and African American "leaders" in particular. Most black leaders recognized Washington's influence and power and were not prepared to risk their careers to challenge him publicly. Moreover, in the late nineteenth and early twentieth centuries none of his critics had developed a comprehensive alternative to his philosophy or approach to the race problem; "a critique that included educational, social, political, and economic strategies to promote blacks' vital interests."

Notwithstanding Du Bois's cordial relationship with Washington at the turn of the century, he slowly began to unmask his concerns about Washington and the Tuskegee model of race relations. In the July 1901 issue of *Dial* magazine Du Bois published a review of Washington's second autobiography, *Up from Slavery*, which was calmly unfavorable to Washington's educational and economic outlook. From this point forward Du Bois became more assertive on the need for African Americans to push for their citizenship rights. In "Hopeful Signs for the Negro," published in October 1902 in *Advance*, he insisted that African Americans would never "abate one jot" from their "determination to attain in this land perfect equality before the law."

Despite these small examples of disagreement, Du Bois and Washington remained cordial; in fact, possibly because of the revelations of his displeasure with Washington's path, there was a new push to court the Atlanta professor to Tuskegee. The principal's powerful trustee, William Henry Baldwin, invited Du Bois to New York to attend a conference on the "condition of the Colored People." While attending the meeting, Baldwin talked to Du Bois about his future and "insisted" that his place "was at Tuskegee." Following the discussion, Du Bois did have two meetings with Washington about the possibility, and he later agreed to speak at Tuskegee in the summer of 1903 as well as work with the principal to gather black leaders to discuss the status and condition of the race. Du Bois was not a silent partner in the relationship. In Saint Paul, Minnesota, in 1902, individuals rose to criticize Washington at a meeting of the Afro-American Council, the nation's only national civil rights organization at the time. The Atlanta professor came to his defense, angering many in the anti-Washington camp. In the pages of his paper, Trotter complained, "We might have expected Prof. Du Bois to have stood in the breach here, but like the others who are trying to get into the band wagon of the Tuskegeean, he is no longer to be relied on."

While all this maneuvering was taking place, a small Chicago publisher, A. C. McClurg, asked Du Bois, who by now had published essays in many of the country's leading black and white periodicals, including *A.M.E. Church Review*, *Colored American*, *New World*, *The Nation*, *Atlantic Monthly*, *The Dial*, *Collier's*, *Booklover's Magazine*, *World Today*, *Outlook*, and *The Independent*, if he would be interested in publishing a collection of essays. He agreed and selected, out of at least three-dozen articles and addresses already written or published, eight essays for adaption or reprinting. In addition, he included five new or "fugitive pieces." Published in April 1903, *The Souls of Black Folk: Essays and Sketches* has become a classic in the English language and one of the most important books of the twentieth century. As one scholar has noted, the collection was "consciously and carefully tailored out of old and new fabric to fit a significant occasion: the first simultaneous appearance of Du Bois as poet, prophet, and scholar, appealing through a long work to the heart and mind of the American nation."

A year after the publication of *Souls* Du Bois admitted that "the style and workmanship" of his book did not make its meaning "altogether clear," although Du Bois revealed himself to be a lyrical, moving, and challenging writer, a master of the essay form. He thought the book conveyed "a clear central message," but around this center floated a shadow of "vagueness and half-veiled allusions." Despite his assessment, the collection sparked a national discussion among black intellectuals. One example was in Chicago, a month after its publication. Ida B. Wells-Barnett and her husband, Ferdinand Barnett, explained that they defended the book's thesis in a literary debate that included Fannie Barrier Williams, S. Laing Williams, and Monroe Work. Three weeks later, Wells-Barnett wrote Du Bois, "We are still reading your book with the same delighted appreciation." Du Bois biographer David Levering Lewis proclaimed that for many African Americans *Souls* was "like fireworks going off in a cemetery . . . sound and light enlivening the inert and the despairing. It was an electrifying manifesto, mobilizing a people for bitter, prolonged struggle to win a place in history."

The Souls of Black Folk, though not directly written in the fashion of reform literature of the period, is akin to the genre's best works. *Souls* is a testament against the rise of the Jim Crow system that had developed from approximately 1890 to 1910. As even arch-racist author Thomas Dixon would say a couple of years after its publication, "His book is a remarkable contribution to the literature of our race problem. In it for the first time we see the naked soul of a Negro beating itself against the bars in which Aryan society has caged him!" "No white man with a soul," he added, "can read this book without a tear." In 1915, Dixon's novel *The Clansman* (1905) would be the basis of the film *The Birth of a Nation* and would go on to inspire the recreation of the Ku Klux Klan.

The "bars" caging the black community were fully visible when *Souls* appeared. The veil of segregation had fallen upon the former Confederacy, where signs indicated segregated railway cars, waiting rooms, restaurants, hotels, wharfs, theaters, and parks. The bulk of southern black males were stripped of their franchise through a variety of nefarious deeds, and in the course of daily human interaction Jim Crow was an assault on the dignity and humanity of the majority of black people throughout the region. The lion's share of southern blacks were sharecroppers, bound to the land as tenants by a cycle of debt, giving half of their crop to the landowner and eking out whatever living they could with the remainder. Those who challenged political and economic oppression frequently met with terrorist violence, "lynch mobs" that were acting largely without the fear of punishment.

Furthermore, in 1903, the Supreme Court upheld disfranchisement laws in *Giles v. Harris*, a case the Afro-American Council and Booker T. Washington, though secretly, had initiated in Alabama, thereby encouraging more states to pass legislation. Finally, in popular culture, Thomas Dixon's play *The Leopard's Spots* (1902), based on a book by the same name, had become the most popular production on Broadway. In this context Du Bois published his collection calling for recognition of African American humanity and contribution to the world. As he would say more than thirty years later in *Black Reconstruction*, African Americans "bent to the storm of beating lynching and murder, and kept their souls in spite of public and private insult of every description; they built an inner culture which the world recognizes in spite of the fact that it is still half-strangled and inarticulate." *The Souls of Black Folk* was Du Bois's first attempt to get the South, the nation, and the world to recognize that "inner culture."

The Souls of Black Folk was "social and cultural history that pleads for recognition of both the suffering and the art in the souls of black folk." On the whole *The Souls of Black Folk* accurately portrayed Du Bois's research scholarship after nearly a decade in the academy—history, sociology, and the spiritual and cultural life of black America. The collection also contains two of Du Bois's most famous assertions. The first was that the problem of the twentieth century was the problem of what he called the "color line." The other is the idea of "double consciousness," a sense of dualism that African Americans possess. While Du Bois often returned to the theme of dualism in *Souls* and other writings throughout his life, he never again used the term "double consciousness."

Through much of the twentieth and early twenty-first centuries, "double consciousness" has become a catchall metaphor for black cultural identity. Many scholars have followed the description of biographer Arnold Rampersad when he explained that double consciousness is about "the inherent and defining condition of the black American who possesses . . . not one but two souls, African and American, perpetually at war within the dark body." In Du Bois's words, "One feels ever his two-ness—an American, a Negro; two souls, two thoughts, two unreconciled strivings." For many scholars over the past fifty years this assertion has come to mean that Du Bois was arguing that there was a constant battle in the black self between American-ness and Negro-ness in the cultural realm. However, scholars such as Ernest Allen Jr. have begun to trouble the waters, challenging the conventional interpretation and arguing that for Du Bois double consciousness was neither a phenomenon that applied to culture, given that Du Bois viewed white and black culture as complementary phenomena, nor, contrary to Du Bois, a paralyzing state that necessarily applied to all black Americans. In terms of duality the fundamental agony lay in the black self's partial internalization of a counterfeit identity imposed by whites; there was also the denial of rights and protections to Americans who also happened to be black. For Du Bois, however, one could be a supporter of all things black and at the same time be an American in its fullest sense.

Even if double consciousness is not the overriding metaphor to understand black culture, *The Souls of Black Folk*, then and today, is a mirror that shows the reader, black or white, the essential form and visage of black America. The first section of the collection, containing "Of Our Spiritual Strivings," "Of the Dawn of Freedom," and "Of Booker T. Washington and Others," addresses history and political theory and sets up the crux of the Atlanta professor's arguments. The first chapter uses history and psychology to argue that the African American population has a past and has something to offer the world. The second chapter reviews black life in Reconstruction and points to the failures of the federal government, in the form of the Freedmen's Bureau, to allow the formerly enslaved to develop to their fullest since emancipation. Finally, the third chapter, which discusses Booker T. Washington, challenges his approach to the race problem and gives lessons for the present and future.

In the middle, and longest, section Du Bois takes the reader behind the veil, one of the important features of the collection. The image of a veil becomes a trope to describe racism to his readers, and in the six chapters that represent the second section of the collection, Du Bois exposes his readers, possibly for the first time, to individuals caught behind the "bars" in which society has "caged" them. As Rampersad has commented, Du Bois's aim was to unmask "the plight of the poor and ignorant, while illuminating their potential for improvement, as well as to defend liberal education for the black man against the sneers of those who argued that 'the picture of a lone black boy poring over a French grammar amid the weeds and dirt of a neglected home' is in many ways 'the acme of absurdities.'"

The final section of *The Souls of Black Folk* focuses on the art, spirituality, and faith of the black community. In "Of the Passing of the First Born," Du Bois bares his soul about the death of his son and reflects on the idea that his son never experienced the tortures of the veil. In "The Faith of the Fathers" he discusses black religion in America. In the final essay, "Of Our Sorrow Songs," he focuses on the melodies of the spirituals and acknowledges that he views the sorrow songs as the example of the black population's "essential capacity for grandeur in thought and expression." Thus, Du Bois ends on a note where he seems to tell his readers that despite what they may have thought before cracking open the book, the citizens of a darker hue are not a national liability, but rather "an unrealized asset in the development of a noble national tradition."

Some contemporaries, and many scholars since, saw the third chapter, "Of Booker T. Washington and Others," as a declaration of war, but Du Bois did not intend it to be a devastating critique, and readers today can see it is not an attack. Du Bois's criticism of Washington's model of leadership constituted a warning shot. It demonstrated frustration but not full-blown contention. Du Bois himself was displeased with Washington's course of action, but he had not come to the point of parting ways with the Wizard of Tuskegee.

In that essay, the Atlanta professor first pays tribute to Washington, especially his ability to bring about a compromise between northern, southern, and African American interests. In doing so, however, Du Bois warns that Washington might have sold short the interests of blacks. Washington's "programme," notes Du Bois, practically accepts the "alleged inferiority of the Negro race," allows economic factors "completely to overshadow the higher aims of life," and preaches a "submission of prejudice." Du Bois furthermore claims that Washington's speeches are filled with "dangerous half truth[s] that the South" used to justify its present attitudes toward African Americans—for example, the position that the future of black Americans depends primarily on their own efforts rather than fair treatment by white Americans. In addition to this paradox, Du Bois notes that while not a "direct result of Mr. Washington's teachings," disfranchisement, greater segregation, increased lynchings, and the withdrawal of aid for black higher education had all followed his ascendancy to power.

While Du Bois may not have seen his essay as a personal attack, the piece has had a profound impact on contemporary and future African American intellectual thought and leadership. Du Bois made public the division in the black community and threatened Washington's claim to leadership. In doing so, he set the terms of the debate for years to come, even if, as has already been stated, their positions on leadership and education were not as wholly incompatible as he made them sound.

As James Weldon Johnson wrote years later, "It is, perhaps, impossible for those unfamiliar with the period to understand the extent of the reaction it caused and the bitterness of the animosities it aroused." *Souls*, according to

Johnson, had a greater impact "upon and within the Negro race than any other single book published in this country since *Uncle Tom's Cabin* (1852)." A decade after its publication, William Farris, a black scholar and ally of William Monroe Trotter, declared *Souls* "the political Bible of the Negro race." He remembered the "thrill and pleasure" of opening the book: "It was an eventful day in my life. It affected me just like Carlyle's 'Heroes and Hero Worship' . . . , Emerson's 'Nature and Other Addresses.' . . . *Souls* came to me as a bolt from the blue. It was the rebellion of a fearless soul, the protest of a noble nature against the blighting American caste prejudice. It proclaimed in thunder tones and in words of magic beauty the worth and sacredness of human personality even when clothed in a black skin."

John Daniels, a white Bostonian social worker, also saw the beauty of the collection and urged others to look beyond the third chapter. He urged readers of *Souls* to judge the collection "not as an argument, as an anti-Washington protest, but as a poem, a spiritual, not an intellectual offering, an appeal not to the head but to the heart." For Daniels, the book deserved the highest praise and admiration, not as "that of a polemic, a transient thing, but that of a poem, a thing permanent."

Souls had a dramatic effect on African American social and political history. Ideological struggles began taking place within the nation's only national civil rights organization, the Afro-American Council, in the late 1890s. The council's supporters included many of the most prominent black political and social elite: Du Bois, Washington, Trotter, Wells-Barnett, and many others were active members. In 1902, when journalist and activist T. Thomas Fortune, an ally of Washington, became president of the organization, many believed it would become a puppet of the Tuskegee sphere and would downplay agitation and the demand for African American civil and political rights.

The following year Du Bois's essay, "Of Booker T. Washington and Others," gave these disagreements legs, and when the organization met in Louisville, Kentucky, for its fifth annual conference, Trotter and his cohorts decided to take a stand against Washington and try to impose their will on the organization. Despite his intentions, Trotter failed miserably. While he was not able to assert any control, his protestations demonstrated that the coalition of pro- and anti-Washington activists that had been carefully cultivated by the Afro-American Council over the first five years of its existence was quickly rotting.

The failure of the organization to secure any legal victories had disappointed many. Supporters both within and without were calling for more sweeping agitation. Moreover, the group's willingness to allow Washington to so publicly dominate the 1902 and 1903 conventions allowed anti-Washington factions to unfairly depict the organization as little more than a puppet representing Washington's unpopular southern strategy. These lapses led to fissures within the coalition. Many had become disillusioned with Washington's strategy and were disturbed because after his ascendency to power the nation continued to fail to uphold black social and civil rights. Such a state of affairs became increasingly frustrating after the Supreme Court's decisions in *Plessy v. Ferguson* (1896) and *Williams v. Mississippi* (1898), cases that strengthened legalized segregation and efforts to disfranchise the southern black electorate, respectively. Because of this feeling of exasperation and the disturbing trend of the nation backpedaling from enforcement of the Fourteenth and Fifteenth Amendments, many activists became more focused on direct agitation to achieve their goals. The seriousness of the situation became apparent right after the Louisville convention, as pro- and anti-Washington forces prepared for a fight.

The publication of *Souls*, the council convention, and Du Bois's post-*Souls* publication in *Booklover's Magazine*, where he implicitly branded the Tuskegeean a political boss, all demonstrated that the gloves were off and a fight loomed. That fight and the action that finally pushed Du Bois firmly into the anti-Washington camp came a few weeks after the Louisville meeting.

Prior to the council convention, Washington had agreed to speak to the Boston branch of the National Negro Business League in late July 1903. As this came only a few weeks after the bumpy convention, tensions remained high. After returning to their homes following the council meeting, William Monroe Trotter and his colleagues kept the criticisms flowing. With Washington's scheduled appearance in "freedom's birthplace" now confirmed, Trotter and his forces planned to seek revenge for their setbacks at Louisville and force the Tuskegee principal to respond to his critics.

On the night of July 30 a capacity crowd filled the Columbus Avenue AME Zion Church. Members of the audience, led by Trotter and Clement Morgan, a Boston lawyer and friend of the *Guardian* editor, disrupted the meeting, causing police to be called to end the disturbance. Four were arrested, and Trotter, one of the four, spent one month in jail, the maximum sentence. The so-called Boston Riot made all the major newspapers, and many in the white and black communities discovered for the first time that Washington had opposition.

Du Bois had no prior knowledge of Trotter's plans and was not in town when the event took place. Ironically, Du Bois was en route from Tuskegee, where he had finished his obligation to teach a summer session, to Boston, where he was scheduled to stay at the Trotters' home for the remainder of the summer. Nina and Yolanda, the Du Boises daughter, had arrived in Boston and were at the Trotters.

Once Du Bois arrived in Boston, though he did not agree with Trotter's tactics, he expressed his opposition to the Boston editor's harsh sentence. As Du Bois stated years later, "When Trotter went to jail, my indignation overflowed. I did not always agree with Trotter then or later. But Trotter was an honest and brilliant, unselfish man, and to treat as crime which was at worst mistaken judgment was an outrage." To back up his sentiment Du Bois published a sympathetic letter he wrote to Trotter shortly after his arrest.

Washington took Du Bois's compassion as proof that he was behind the "conspiracy to riot." In October he wrote to Robert C. Ogden, an owner of Wanamaker's department store in Philadelphia and a major supporter of black education, falsely stating that he had "evidence which is indisputable showing that Dr. Du Bois is very largely behind the mean and underhanded attacks that have been made upon me." In the end Washington had no proof against Du Bois, but he succeeded in alerting northern philanthropists to avoid making donations to Atlanta University. In addition, one by one, Washington's opponents began losing political appointments and jobs as he flexed his political muscles and pulled strings behind the scenes.

Washington claimed victory, but the Boston Riot of 1903 represented a turning point in African American history. For Du Bois the argument against Washington was not only about disagreements on emphasis of particular approaches to the race problem. The differences with the Tuskegeean had become questions of principle. The movement from *Souls* to *Booklover's* to the fallout from the Boston fray had been dramatic. The two, however, continued to work together on the proposed conference in New York to discuss race issues. For most of the remainder of the year they negotiated over whom to invite as delegates, and the conference convened in Carnegie Hall on January 6, 1904. After the remarks of a few white supporters, who had been invited by Washington, the Tuskegee principal officially opened the proceedings with an address asking for the delegation to understand the precarious situation within which he lived in the South. Du Bois followed the Wizard by stating that there could be no compromise on African Americans' civil and political rights, higher education, and public accommodation. The Atlanta professor insisted, furthermore, that Washington cease and desist making public comments that made blacks the butt of humor and ridicule.

Three days of heated discussion followed, as well as persuasive closing addresses by both Du Bois and Washington. Afterward the delegation agreed on a program containing eight resolutions covering migration, suffrage, segregation, lynching, education, and race relations in general, as well as specifically southern conditions and the dissemination of information to the general public. The group also endorsed the necessity of spreading "knowledge of the truth in regard to all matters affecting the race." Finally, it called for the creation of a "Committee of Safety with twelve members" (Committee of Twelve) to serve as a bureau of information and to "seek to unify and bring into cooperation the action of the various organizations" throughout the nation.

After the meeting, with both factions claiming victory, conferees dispersed throughout the nation ready to work with their respective organizations and uphold the principles set forth by the delegation. The Committee of Twelve was so packed with Tuskegee supporters, however, that Du Bois resigned within six months and urged Archibald Grimké, a Boston-based lawyer and activist, and Kelly Miller, a sociologist, essayist, and activist, to do the same. The committee continued, but it never became what it could have been; the fissures had become too much to prevent the group from splitting apart.

Throughout 1904, Du Bois became increasingly vocal in his criticism of Washington. In both articles and speeches he was more outspoken on the issue of Washington's character and methods. For instance, one year after the publication of *The Souls of Black Folk*, which went through three printings in its first eight months, he published an article in *The World To-Day* titled "Parting the Ways." The article was a damaging criticism of Washington and constituted more of a signal break with the Tuskegeean than had Du Bois's *Souls* essay, "Of Booker T. Washington and Others," as the title clearly indicated. Juxtaposing Washington's leadership and racial philosophy with that of the great black leaders of the past, the Atlanta professor now concluded that the Tuskegee principal stood in historical as well as moral opposition to older leaders such as Bishop Daniel Payne, Alexander Crummell, T. Thomas Fortune, and Frederick Douglass. According to Du Bois, none of these individuals could have supported Washington's position, as they had "fought for the highest education available," and they understood that it was "impossible for free workingmen without the ballot to compete with free workingmen who have the ballot." Moreover, these leaders of the past understood that blacks would become free only if they had "the courage and persistence to demand the rights and treatment of men and to cease to toady and apologize and belittle themselves." Du Bois therefore called on African Americans to "refuse to kiss the hand that smites us" and to "insist on striving by all civilized methods to keep wide educational opportunity, to keep the right to vote, to insist on equal civil rights and to gain every right and privilege open to a free American citizen."

Hostilities between Du Bois and Washington increased in early 1905. In a brief essay for the Atlanta publication *The Voice of the Negro*, Du Bois offhandedly remarked that Tuskegee had spent at least $3,000 in bribes to the black press the previous year to silence Washington's enemies. Because this accusation implied that Washington had even less support than some in the white and black communities believed, that instead he was purchasing silence and support, the Tuskegee Machine was quick to respond. The Tuskegee Machine used the incident to smear Dr. Du Bois. T. Thomas Fortune's paper labeled him "Professor of hysterics." Moreover, when Du Bois was asked to provide evidence by Oswald Garrison Villard, editor of the *New York Evening Post* and grandson of abolitionist William Lloyd Garrison, he failed to provide more than hearsay, mostly from Trotter and his allies. Villard chastised Du Bois and questioned his reliance on individuals such as Trotter.

Professor Du Bois, however, had increasingly been forging alliances with anti-Bookerites like Trotter since the publication of *Souls*, and for him the press subsidy issue was the last straw. He and the increasing anti-Washington crowd moved toward establishing their own organization. During the summer of 1905, Du Bois secretly sent a circular proposing a meeting of a few dozen race leaders. "The time seems," he asserted, "more than ripe for organized, determined and aggressive action on the part of men who believe in Negro freedom and growth." He called on those receiving the circular to meet during the summer for the following purposes:

1. To oppose firmly the present methods of strangling honest criticism, manipulating public opinion and centralizing political power by means of the improper and corrupt use of money and influence.

2. To organize thoroughly the intelligent and honest Negroes throughout
   the United States for the purpose of insisting on manhood rights, industrial opportunity and spiritual freedom.
3. To establish proper organs of news and public opinion.

Although the call went out under Du Bois's name, the creation of the new
group was a collaborative effort. As the Atlanta professor himself noted,
"The honor of founding the organization belongs to F. L. McGhee, who first
suggested it; C. C. Bentley, who planned the method of organization and W.
M. Trotter, who put the backbone into the platform." Approximately a month
after Du Bois and his colleagues distributed the letter, twenty-nine race men
converged on Buffalo, New York, and Fort Erie, Ontario, on the Canadian
side of Niagara Falls to discuss the proposed organization.

During the four-day event the participants quibbled over the wording of
the new group's "Declaration of Principles," but the attendees all agreed that
they had traveled to the Niagara Falls region to create an organization that
thoroughly stood for the manhood rights of African Americans. Though
many of the delegates openly opposed Washington's racial philosophy, Du
Bois made it clear that opposition to the Wizard was not the reason he had
called the delegation to the site. According to J. Max Barber, a delegate from
Atlanta and editor of the *Voice of the Negro*, Du Bois insisted "We have
gathered to discuss principles not men. If Mr. Washington can subscribe to
the principles he will be welcomed as a member of the Niagara Movement. If
he cannot, that is his business."

As Barber explained, the new movement sought "to reinstitute ideals in
human behavior for the white man as well as the black." Those in the Niagara
Movement believed, he asserted, "that it is better for the Negro to be a man
with a man's spirit and a man's intellectual and moral stature than that he
should be a coward with any amount of thrift and energy." The delegates
concurred with Barber's enunciation of the philosophy of the new movement, and after three full days of discussion agreed upon the structure of the
new organization and its basic principles. The platform, written in sharp
tones by William Monroe Trotter and W. E. B. Du Bois, consisted of eight
basic demands setting forth the position of the new civil rights group. The
members of the Niagara Movement insisted upon:

> freedom of speech and criticism, an unfettered and unsubsidized press, full
> manhood suffrage, abolition of segregation, recognition of human brotherhood
> as a practical present creed, recognition of the highest and best education as

the monopoly of no race or class, belief in the dignity of labor, and united effort to realize these ideals under wise and courageous leadership.

After approving the Declaration of Principles, the delegation agreed upon a constitution for the new group based on an outline drafted for the Committee of Twelve by Du Bois and submitted to Washington in early 1904. The Niagara Movement's general organizational structure was also reminiscent of its Afro-American League and Council counterparts. The basic structure of the organization consisted of state associations: sixteen states plus the District of Columbia at its inception. The chairmen of the state associations made up the group's executive committee and were led by the general secretary (Du Bois was the first to hold the position). Finally, the following committees were established: Finance, Interstate Conditions and Needs, Organization, Civil and Political Rights, Legal Defense, Crime, Rescue and Reform, Economic Opportunity, Health, Education, Press, and Public Opinion.

Following the opening meeting of the Niagara Movement, Washington attempted to limit the flow of publicity concerning the new civil rights organization. In seeking to gather as much information about the movement prior to its inception, the Wizard had unsuccessfully tried to spy on the conference proceedings. Washington clearly viewed the movement as a threat and sought to isolate the group by encouraging a media blackout of its proceedings.

At the meeting, despite Du Bois's efforts to suppress criticisms of Washington, the Niagara Movement's very existence provided an implicit critique of the Wizard's program as well as an introduction of an alternative path. Many of the members of the Niagara Movement were essentially Trotterites who had sought to challenge Washington since 1902. Moreover, sentiments expressing the movement's Declaration of Principles—for example, that the race needs "leadership and is given cowardice and apology"—could only be read as a direct challenge to Washington's leadership.

Despite Washington's attempts to isolate the new organization, by the end of 1905 it claimed nearly 150 members and seventeen state branches. In its first year of activity, however, it did little in the way of concrete action, and in many ways mirrored the organization and activities of the three other national civil rights organizations, the Afro-American Council, the Committee of Twelve, and the Constitution League, so much so that many in the African American community were calling for unification of all the groups to consolidate the effort. A merger, however, did not yet happen, and the Niagarites pushed forward on their own with forty-five of them meeting in late August 1906 at Storer College in Harpers Ferry, West Virginia. The second convention's proceedings were drenched in symbolism as the event opened with the delegates singing "Battle Hymn of the Republic" and "John Brown's Body." A day was devoted to the honor of John Brown, with a lengthy tributary address by the Reverend Reverdy Ransom, who was accompanied on stage by, among others, Lewis Douglass, son of Frederick Douglass; Mrs. Evans, the aunt of John Copeland, a Brown supporter who was also put to death after the raid on the armory; and William Monroe Trotter, who presented the delegation with a piece of wood from Brown's Springfield, Massachusetts, home, which he had collected on his trip from Boston.

The conference was full of fanfare, but overall the organization had not done much in its first year of existence. Two events would occur in 1906, however, that would invigorate members of the movement and the other civil rights organizations as well as weaken Booker T. Washington's program and leadership: the Atlanta Riot and the Brownsville Affair.

On the night of August 13, 1906, a group of armed men "shot up" the town of Brownsville, Texas. During the disturbance one person was killed and two others were wounded. Before the incident racial tensions had been on the rise in the area between black soldiers stationed at Fort Brown and whites in Brownsville due to racial discrimination the soldiers experienced while stationed in the region. Following the riot, local military investigation concluded that black soldiers, members of the Twenty-Fifth Infantry, were the culprits, even though the identities of the gunmen were never established. The incident infuriated members of the national civil rights organizations, and when President Roosevelt, a friend of Booker T. Washington, dishonorably discharged the soldiers with seemingly no protest from the Tuskegee principal, the community lost faith in the Wizard and his leadership.

A few short weeks after Brownsville and a couple of months before President Roosevelt's decisive action in the affair, the streets of the South's ideal example for the new southern race relations ran with blood. Atlanta, Georgia, the southern city that many believed to be the model for the New South, became the site of a deadly riot in late summer 1906. The simultaneous sounding of the fire alarm, riot call, and militia muster shattered the calm Saturday evening. Racial tensions had been on the rise in the city for a number of months, spurred by the Hoke Smith disfranchisement gubernatorial campaign, allegations of African American criminal activity, and the recent theatrical production of Thomas Dixon's *The Clansman*. Tensions continued to escalate until they could no longer be contained, and they ferociously exploded upon the city. On Saturday evening, mobs struck out at any African American who unfortunately happened upon their path, killing a number of innocent blacks.

Sunday was ominously quiet, and the pall that hung in the air exploded the following day. Occasionally reinforced by police, the mobs focused their renewed energy on the southeastern portion of the city. The mob directed much of its anger toward schools, businesses, and homes of law-abiding citizens of the community. African Americans attempting to protect themselves and their property exchanged gunfire with the white mobs. In the end, property damage exceeded thousands of dollars, while ten African Americans died and sixty people were hospitalized.

Du Bois was out of town doing research, but he immediately returned to Atlanta. Fear for his family and images of the town that he had praised three years earlier in his essay "Of the Wings of Atlanta," published in *The Souls of Black Folk*, mixed in his head. Perhaps he recalled the lines of John Greenleaf Whittier's poem "Howard at Atlanta," which he had used for the epigraph of that essay:

> O black boy of Atlanta!
> But Half was spoken;
> The slave's chains and the master's
> Alike are broken
> The one curse of the races
> Held both in tether;
> They are rising—all are rising—
> The black and the white together.

The Atlanta professor wondered what had gone wrong, and in response composed the "Litany of Atlanta":

> Listen to us, Thy children; our faces dark with doubt, are made a
> mockery in Thy sanctuary. With uplifted hands we front Thy heaven,
> O God, crying: we beseech Thee to hear us, good Lord! . . . Surely, Thou
> too art not white, O Lord a pale, bloodless, heartless, thing? . . . But
> whisper—speak—call, great God, for Thy silence is white terror to our
> hearts!

Booker T. Washington, in contrast to many within the various civil rights organizations, urged the black community to practice restraint and said that a biracial organization was needed in Atlanta to create better race relations. His actions and comments around the two incidents in 1906 caused many to question his leadership. The violence of the riot and the dishonorable discharge of the soldiers, coupled with the reaction of white northerners to both outrages, made a growing group understand that the North and South shared the same views of blacks and that no political compromise would change these attitudes. The call for protest and agitation from Du Bois, Trotter, and Alexander Walters, the president of the Afro-American Council, now made more sense than Washington's call for a compromise.

Despite this transformation, the Niagara Movement and the other existing civil rights organizations were not the groups that the community used to gain larger protest victories in the future. After convening for three more annual conferences, the Niagara Movement folded up its tents. Always in financial difficulty, plagued with organizational problems and personality conflicts, and constantly challenged by Washington and his allies, the Niagara Movement limped along from the beginning. The Niagara Movement, however, along with the other civil rights organizations of the period, the Afro-American Council, and the Constitution League, kept the aggressive and unconditional demand for African American civil and political rights alive and laid the foundation for the NAACP.

In late summer 1908 there was a race riot in Springfield, Illinois, and many throughout the nation were shocked that such an incident would occur in the hometown of Abraham Lincoln. A number of white liberals and many African Americans who had been "voicing protest" for decades, including Du Bois, met at the 1909 National Negro Conference to discuss the need to organize a unified group to advocate for the civil rights of African Americans. The following year the activists present at the conference and their supporters formalized the creation of the NAACP, and Du Bois joined the group's leadership as the director of research and publications and the editor of the new national journal, *The Crisis*.

The new position was not without risk. While the position offered him a salary of $2,500, double what he earned at Atlanta University, the job was only guaranteed for a year. The move was necessary, however. The transition allowed him to get his family out of the South, which he and especially Nina wanted after the Atlanta Riot. He was also feeling stymied professionally in Atlanta and was beginning to look for a new direction. Washington noticed this transition after the creation of the Niagara Movement and averred, "When [Du Bois] stuck to the business of scientific investigation he was a success." But the professor was, Washington observed, moving into civil rights activism, and he predicted he would be "a failure as an agitator" and would "make a fool of himself." The Wizard of Tuskegee was correct in his observation but mistaken in his prediction.

During the first few years of the new century Dr. Du Bois had become more of a political actor than in the first ten-odd years of his professional life. This transition was not entirely to his liking. He felt that he was producing too much propaganda and not enough scientific research. With considerable difficulty he attempted to maintain his social science research projects, particularly his Atlanta studies. In addition he continued to write popular essays on race relations for various white and black periodicals. In 1904, he submitted a piece to *The Nation* on the decline of "Negro illiteracy," and a couple of years later *Collier's* published "The Color Line Belts the World," which further expanded upon his famous argument in 1900, repeated in *Souls*, that the "problem of the twentieth century was the color-line." Finally in 1910, he published "The Souls of White Folk" in *The Independent*. Sitting upon his perch in Atlanta, Du Bois explained, he had become perplexed by those "souls . . . that have become painfully conscious of their whiteness." He observed that racism had produced the powerful common computation in white minds: "I am white and you are black. . . . I am white and you are nothing." Despite its utter absurdity, white Americans had consistently "suppressed evidence, misquoted authority, distorted fact and deliberately lied. It is wonderful," he quipped, "that in the very lines of social study, where America should shine, it has done nothing."

In addition to his sociological work of the period Du Bois produced some works of political and social history as well as some literary pieces. In the Atlanta-based journal the *Voice of the Negro*, he published a four-part series on the history of slavery. He also published a path-breaking essay on the subject of Reconstruction, "Reconstruction and Its Benefits," where he highlighted the success of state governments during the period, including the creation of public schools, political rights for all citizens, and social welfare legislation. It would take nearly fifty years for the historical profession to catch up with Du Bois's analysis.

His longest historical piece of the first decade of the new century was a biography of John Brown. Du Bois had initially wanted to write a biography of Frederick Douglass for George W. Jacobs and Company's biographical series, but he was informed that Booker T. Washington was given that subject. Then after the press rejected his second choice of 1831 Southampton,

Virginia, slave revolt leader Nat Turner, he settled on the abolitionist and leader of the 1859 raid on the federal armory in Harpers Ferry, West Virginia. Dr. Du Bois began writing the biography the year he helped organize the Niagara Movement, but the book was not published for another four years.

One of Du Bois's lasting and influential pieces of the period was the "Credo," a prose poem first published in *The Independent* in October 1904, at the same time he was beginning to assert himself more directly into the national discussion of which direction the African American community should go. In the piece he affirmed his belief in God, humanity, and civil rights and called upon the community and the nation as a whole to adopt this manifesto. It outlined his hopes, a world without war, the "training of Children," the achievement of political liberty "for all men: the space to stretch their arms and their souls, the right to breathe and the right to vote." The simple piece, designed in a way that asked the community to respond using the call-and-response tradition of the African American church, was republished numerous times and became a memorization exercise for black youth and a frequently framed page in African American homes throughout the country.

In spite of all his continued production on the literary, scientific, and historical fronts by 1910, Du Bois had become convinced that "not simply knowledge, not simply direct repression of evil, will reform the world." Furthermore, he noted, "first, one could not be a calm, cool, and detached scientist while Negroes were lynched, murdered, and starved; and secondly, there was no such definite demand for scientific work of the sort I was doing, as I had confidently assumed would be easily forthcoming." For these reasons and more, Du Bois resigned from Atlanta University in 1910 to take a position as director of publications and research for the newly formed NAACP. This move from Atlanta to New York, from the ivory tower to the editorial office of *The Crisis*, the new organization's organ, would have a profound effect on the man, the black community, and the nation as a whole. For it is in this capacity as editor of *The Crisis* that Du Bois became the individual that many look back on so fondly today. It was in this new role that he transformed from an academic to the voice of the community. As he explained, "My career as a scientist was to be swallowed up in my role as master of propaganda." By 1915, as the new magazine's circulation skyrocketed and Booker T. Washington passed away, Du Bois became "the most prominent prophet of the Negro race."

Chapter Four

Building Movement

The NAACP, Pan-Africanism, Garvey, and a Renaissance

Then came *The Crisis*, like a clear, strong breeze cutting through the miasma of Negrophobism. Here for the first time with brilliance, militancy, facts, photographs and persuasiveness, a well-edited magazine challenged the whole concept of white supremacy then nationally accepted. . . . It is no exaggeration to say that the early *Crisis* created an intellectual revolution in the most out-of-way places. . . . It became the bible of the militant Negro of the day and "must" reading for the growing numbers of his white champions.

          —George S. Schuyler (1951)

The NAACP formed in the aftermath of a race riot in Springfield, Illinois, in August 1908. While neither the first nor the last racial pogrom in America's racial history, this act of racial violence—which left two blacks lynched, four whites killed, and more than seventy people injured—sparked indignation and shock among black and white reformers because it took place not only in the North, but in the hometown of Abraham Lincoln. William English Walling, a young journalist who investigated the riot, along with social workers Henry Moskowitz, Mary White Ovington, and Oswald Garrison Villard, a newspaper editor and grandson of abolitionist William Lloyd Garrison, soon after called a meeting to join in a national conference to discuss "present evils, the voicing of protest, and the renewal of the struggle for civil and political liberty." This National Negro Conference, considered the founding meeting of the NAACP although the organization adopted its official name a year later, was held in New York City on May 31 and June 1, 1909. The majority of those attending the conference were white philanthropists and social reformers, but black participants included Ida B. Wells-Barnett, William Monroe Trotter, Alexander Walters, William Sinclair, and W. E. B. Du Bois, all of whom had spearheaded previous African American protests and were prominent members of the more than two-decade-old struggle in the African American community to create a national civil rights organization. Programmatically, the new organization vigorously opposed racial hatred and prejudice, promising not to shy away from fully exposing the squalid veracity regarding the treatment of African Americans in the United States.

William English Walling asked Du Bois to work full-time for the new organization on June 8, 1910. Du Bois, wanting to continue his research and writing career, replied to Walling with a question regarding his potential duties and the resources available to carry them out. "In looking over your budget it occurs to me," Du Bois stated, "that no provision is made for research work, unless something is included under postage." Du Bois, after subsequent negotiations, agreed to join the new group as the only African American on the executive committee and the director of publications and research.

Du Bois served as the editor of the group's new journal, *The Crisis: A Record of the Darker Races*, named after a James Russell Lowell poem, "The Present Crisis." As the editor, Du Bois crafted himself into an expert propagandist. His mastery of persuasion in printed prose was clear in the debut issue of the magazine, published on November 1, 1910. As Du Bois explained, the magazine's object was to "set forth those facts and arguments which show the danger of race prejudice, particularly manifested to-day toward colored people." He further outlined that *The Crisis* would "first and foremost be a newspaper," reporting on events and movements that "bear on the great problem of inter-racial relations." However, it would also review literature dealing with racial questions, respond to opinions of race relations offered in other publications, and publish short articles, while "its editorial page will stand for the right of men, irrespective of color or race, for the highest ideals of American democracy, and for reasonable but earnest and persistent attempts to gain these rights and realize these ideals."

Headquartered in downtown Manhattan, *The Crisis* became Du Bois's voice as well as the main propaganda outlet for the NAACP. In his position as editor of *The Crisis* the author of the now-classic works *The Philadelphia*

Negro and *The Souls of Black Folk* honed his craft and became the scholar-activist so revered today. "With *The Crisis*," he explained, "I essayed a new role of interpreting to the world the hindrances and aspirations of American Negroes. My older program appeared only as I supported my contention with facts from current reports and observation or historic reference. My writing was reinforced by lecturing, and my knowledge increased by travel."

Du Bois and the NAACP launched *The Crisis* at a critical "psychological moment"; less than fifty years after emancipation and during a time when discrimination had become entrenched nationally and was sanctioned by science, law, and public opinion. In spite of the discouraging moment in time, or perhaps because of it, the magazine became a remarkable success. Circulation rose from 1,000 for the first issue to several thousand within a few months. By 1917, its readership had grown to 50,000, expanding to more than 100,000 two years later in 1919. As a result, the readership of *The Crisis*, a diverse group but driven largely by the growing black middle class, surpassed that of popular, well-known magazines such as the *New Republic* and *The Nation*. As Du Bois and the leadership of the civil rights organization conceived, the magazine was the voice of the NAACP. The stories and editorials in its pages informed the readers of the activities of the organization on both the national and local levels, giving greater cohesion to the organization as a whole. Moreover, Du Bois pushed his readers to become members of the organization, as he did in 1914 when he screamed from the pages: "Join the NATIONAL ASSOCIATION FOR THE ADVANCEMENT OF COLORED PEOPLE or be strangled to a slow and awful death by growing prejudice." But with his ever-sharpening pen, *The Crisis* also became a personal journal, an extension of Du Bois and his agenda as he sought to educate the world on race issues and to mold, join, and uplift the race politically, culturally, and spiritually.

Du Bois's control of *The Crisis* often ruffled the feathers of fellow NAACP board members. The first conflict came with the organization's chairman, Oswald Garrison Villard, who wanted greater oversight of the journal. He was a major force in creating the NAACP, especially the founding group, the National Negro Committee. Moreover, he himself was the publisher of the *Evening Post* and *The Nation* and was lending office space for the magazine. These facts certainly would have led Villard to believe he would have more involvement in the content and direction of the magazine. When he failed to gain more control, he tried to undermine Du Bois by questioning whether the organization was getting its money's worth from the doctor. While editing *The Crisis*, Du Bois had kept up a rigorous research, writing, and lecturing schedule outside of the pages of the magazine and the organization. In the first five years of the organization he published pieces in the *New York Times*, *Boston Globe*, *Atlantic Monthly*, and *The Independent*. Du Bois also contributed important historical essays, "Reconstruction and Its Benefits" and "The Economics of Negro Emancipation," in the *American Historical Review* and the *Sociological Review*, respectively. Moreover, he gave seventy-two lectures in 1913 and forty-five in 1914.

Du Bois saw this activity as his own time as long as *The Crisis* and the message of the NAACP were still being published to the best of his ability and on time. Moreover, Du Bois forwarded half the subscription rate, $1, to the organization's treasury. Villard felt that Du Bois was not giving enough attention to *The Crisis* and questioned the amount of the subscription rate he was turning over to the organization's coffers. The chairman tried to get members of the board to decrease Du Bois's control of the magazine but failed to gain their full support. As the relationship between the editor and the chairman continued to deteriorate, Villard even asked for his name to be removed from the masthead of the magazine and in 1915 threatened to have his wealthy friends turn their backs on the organization. "My name has brought in a good deal of money from people who give liberally because of their faith in me," he purred, "and I cannot be in that position of trust and see *The Crisis* conducted as it is." Despite his protests, Villard never wrestled control of *The Crisis* from Du Bois, and he resigned from the chairmanship in 1913, to be replaced by Joel Spingarn, a wealthy former Columbia University professor.

Du Bois, on the other hand, kept moving forward. He continued to shape *The Crisis* to educate the nation, both within and outside the black community. He saw *The Crisis* as the tool creating the seeds for a larger movement for civil rights. Du Bois considered his readership "as soil being prepared for seed of permanent organization." As historian Elliott Rudwick explained, "The journal was the grand mentor of the race—it alone could teach Negroes not only how to protest *but how to live*. After colored Americans had received sufficient indoctrination from the *Crisis* 'branch,' they would be better able to fit into the NAACP branch."

Du Bois's competitors in the black press also felt the growth, success, and influence of *The Crisis*. Many saw *The Crisis* and Du Bois as a threat because the success of his magazine perceivably meant fewer subscriptions for themselves, and his editorial approach often made them seem more moderate or out of touch with the issues of the day. William Calvin Chase, the editor of the influential *Washington Bee*, complained that the NAACP was supplementing *The Crisis* with its membership dues and therefore creating an unfair advantage for Du Bois and his magazine. Du Bois responded to this concern by pointing out, *"The Crisis* supports itself, and has from the beginning." He continued by expressing regret and disdain, arguing that what was worthy of reprinting in *The Crisis* by the black press was limited because the editors of the African American weekly newspapers gave more "careful attention to some of the very things which this editor denounces [to] bring larger success" to their own papers. Du Bois also criticized the black press for its frequent inability to provide adequate facts, failure to use proper English, and lack of principles.

The Crisis and its editor were bold and uncompromising and set a very high standard. As sociologist Ellen Irene Diggs noted, "Du Bois analyzed, interpreted, denounced, condemned what he believed was wrong whether perpetuated by president, royalty, or commoner." From the opening issue, the range of topics to which Du Bois and his staff introduced their readers were broad and diverse. Distinguished authors including Franz Boas, H. L. Mencken, E. Franklin Frazier, Oswald Garrison Villard, Zora Neale Hurston, Arthur Schomburg, Charles Chesnutt, Walter White, Benjamin G. Brawley, William Pickens, James Weldon Johnson, Fenton Johnson, and Langston Hughes published articles, critiques, and poetry in the pages of *The Crisis*. In addition to the diverse collection of material Du Bois selected for *The Crisis*, he dedicated special issues to the topics of women, children, and education every year.

Lynching and mob violence, however, became the most common theme discussed in the magazine. From 1909 to 1918, there were 687 lynchings in America, and 590 of the victims were African American. Through writing, photographs, and sketches, Du Bois shed light on these ghastly acts of unprosecuted murder occurring throughout the nation. During this period some form of the word *lynching* appeared on nearly two thousand different pages of *The Crisis*. In 1916, Du Bois, building on the pioneering efforts of Ida B. Wells-Barnett, began publishing "The Lynching Industry," a record of the individuals lynched and the reasons given for their murder. Additionally, in July 1916, Du Bois published a supplementary issue of *The Crisis* on the brutal Waco, Texas, lynching, which included the gruesome images of the charred remains of Jesse Washington, the African American teenager murdered on May 15, 1916. Du Bois believed that Washington's burning was so

brutal and outrageous that a special issue was necessary and that the publication of the horrific images of the burned remains would shake the consciousness of the nation. In many ways the special issue on the Washington lynching became a precursor to the actions taken by the Johnson Publication
Company when it printed the images of Emmett Till's battered body in *Jet
Magazine* in September 1955.

In addition to these themes and issues, Du Bois supported copious other
causes in *The Crisis*. Du Bois was an advocate for women's suffrage and
African independence and a strong advocate for Pan-Africanism and the
rights of labor. From his columns titled "Opinions," "Editorials," "The Bur-
den," "Along the Colored Line," "The Looking Glass," "Postscripts," "As
the Crow Flies," and "The Horizon," Du Bois condemned presidents,
governors, judges, and colleagues and friends when he thought they were in
the wrong. The Republican and Democratic parties, unions, public health
service, the Census Bureau, the War Department, the Department of Justice,
and the white and black church all felt the sting of his sharp language.

The Crisis, and Du Bois as its editor, were revolutionary. Combining
social science research, literary and artistic production, history, and opinion
the editor and the NAACP used the magazine to try to drastically change the
way whites and blacks thought about themselves and each other. A *Rich-
mond Times-Dispatch* editorial of January 12, 1914, demonstrated just how
revolutionary and shocking *The Crisis* was for the nation.

> Someone has sent us a special number of a Negro monthly magazine, which
> appears to us to be about the most incendiary document that has passed
> through the mails since the anarchists' literature was barred. . . . This particular
> magazine is of limited circulation, and is probably the organ of ambitious
> Negroes in New York. Its remarks, therefore, are scarcely worthy of consider-
> ation and its opinions beneath notice. But were this spirit to spread among the
> Negroes, we can but think how disastrous would be its workings.

For more than two decades Du Bois and *The Crisis* challenged the black
community and the nation as a whole. As he explained, "We are trying
something which has not often been done, that is to spread propaganda over a
wide space where there is no territorial unity. We are trying to bring together
people who have never seen each other, but simply have racial discrimination
as a point of contact." *The Crisis* under the editorial guidance of Du Bois
trained future activists. "We can piddle on," Du Bois argued to Joel Spingarn, "we can do a few, small obvious things, but the great blow—the freeing

of ten million and of the other millions who they pull down—that means power and organization on a tremendous scale. The men who will fight in these ranks must be educated and *The Crisis* can train them, not simply in its words, but in its manner, its pictures, its conception of life."

As *The Crisis*, Du Bois, and the NAACP were gaining influence in the mid-to-late 1910s, Booker T. Washington passed away. Despite their continued tension-filled relationship after the Boston Riot and the creation of the Niagara Movement and the NAACP, Du Bois published a tasteful obituary of the Tuskegee principal in December 1915. While he did reiterate his belief that Washington's conciliatory approach had done damage to race relations and allowed the expansion of segregation and disfranchisement, he also praised him for bringing the attention of African Americans "to the pressing necessity of economic development." Du Bois also asserted that Washington "was the greatest Negro leader since Frederick Douglass, and the most distinguished man, white or black, who has come out of the South since the Civil War."

With Washington's passing, however, Du Bois and the NAACP moved to bring the race leadership together and establish their primacy as the leaders of the civil rights struggle. Joel Spingarn, urged by Du Bois, called fifty men and one woman to his home in Amenia, New York, for a three-day conference in August 1916 to, according to Du Bois, "gloss over hurts and enmities" and "to bring about as large a degree as possible of unity of purpose among Negro leaders." In essence the idea was to find common ground and advance the "position that all can agree upon."

The three days included discussions and breaks to play "good and hard," according to Du Bois; all enjoyed a good bit of swimming, rowing, hiking, flower picking, and singing. The conferees discovered that none "held uncompromising and unchangeable views. It was all a matter of emphasis." "We all believed in thrift," explained Du Bois, "we all wanted the Negro to vote, we all wanted the laws enforced, we all wanted assertion of our essential manhood; but how to get these things—there of course was infinite divergence of opinion." The attendees therefore resolved to work in unity; put aside their "outdated suspicions and factional alignments"; push for all forms of education and the vote; and understand that black leaders in the South lived under special circumstances.

A decade later, Du Bois recalled that the conference "not only marked the end of the old things and the old thoughts and the old ways of attacking the race problem, but in addition to this it was the beginning of the new things.

Probably on account of our meeting the Negro race was more united and more ready to meet the problems of the work than it could possibly have been." Fred Moore, editor of the *New York Age* and an attendee at the conference, concurred, as he stated directly after Amenia, "It marks the birth of a new spirit of united purpose and effort that will have far-reaching results."

Some historians have disagreed, however, asserting that the conference's influence and transformative nature have been exaggerated. In spite of this, what is evident is that Du Bois and the NAACP were the victors of the Amenia Conference. Following the meeting, the NAACP solidified its position of primacy in the fight for African American rights after Booker T. Washington's death, and at the center of this growing organization were Du Bois and *The Crisis*. The development of the NAACP was also aided by the association's hiring of James Weldon Johnson as national organizer and field secretary. Born in Jacksonville, Florida, in 1871, Johnson had served in the State Department from 1905 to 1913 as an American consul in Venezuela and Nicaragua. He was also a well-known author of poetry, many articles, and the novel *The Autobiography of an Ex-Colored Man* (1912).

Johnson's legwork and Du Bois's pen worked hand-in-hand to transform the NAACP into a national civil rights organization. When Johnson joined the group in 1916, it contained about 70 branches and 9,000 members. By 1918, due in large part to Johnson's fieldwork, the organization included 165 branches and 44,000 members. In 1920, that number had risen to 62,000, and the NAACP was the most influential black organization in America.

While Du Bois was honing his editorial craft in *The Crisis* every month and leading the race on the domestic front, he never relinquished his interest in international affairs and the darker peoples of the world. In 1909, Du Bois outlined the creation of an "Encyclopedia Africana covering the chief points in the history and condition of the Negro race." In 1911 he traveled to London to participate in the Universal Races Conference, and in 1915 Du Bois published a pioneering work on the history of the role of African people in world history, called *The Negro*.

Written for the Home University Library series, *The Negro* constituted Du Bois's first attempt at challenging the opinion that Africa had no history worth respecting until Europeans made contact with the continent. Elements of his argument were made nearly twenty years before when he delivered his "Conservation of the Races" address before the American Negro Academy and in scattered works over the years, but with this book he tried to assemble a succinct but comprehensive volume that demonstrated Africa's and

Africans' integral part in human history. Africans and their descendants have been just as capable in their achievements as people of European descent. In the work, consisting of twelve chapters, eight on Africa and the remainder on slavery and the Diaspora's experience in the New World, Du Bois, among other points, "popularized the history of African kingdoms" and argued that African slavery did not destroy all aspects of traditional African culture.

Countering popular discourse, Du Bois asserted that African achievement, and that of Africans in the Diaspora, was a result of their own ingenuity. "Effort has naturally," Du Bois asserted, "been made to ascribe this civilization to white people." Proclaiming all the theories "far-fetched," he continued, "If ever a people exhibited unanswerable evidence of indigenous civilization, it is the west-coast Africans. Undoubtedly they adapted much that came to them, utilized new ideas, and grew from contact. But their art and culture is Negro through and through."

Du Bois then hypothesized that European civilization grew from African origins. At the same time he pulled back on the racial concept, repeating the argument of "The Conservation of the Races." It "is generally recognized today that no scientific definition of race is possible," wrote Du Bois, echoing a then-radical idea that has since become orthodoxy. Only the historical and "spiritual" distinctions are useful. "Race is a dynamic and not a static conception, and the typical races are continually changing and developing, amalgamating and differentiating," he argued. In *The Negro*, Du Bois asserted that he was "studying the history of the darker part of the human family, which is separated from the rest of mankind by no absolute physical line, but which nevertheless forms, as a mass, a social group distinct in history, appearance, and to some extent in spiritual gift."

Du Bois pointed to indigenous elements of high civilization at nearly every point in time and space. By every gauge of culture—agriculture, industry, music, sculpture, and other forms of creative expression as well as in forms of social and political organization—Du Bois argued that Africa met the highest standards. Analogously to points he had emphasized in "The Conservation of Races" and *The Souls of Black Folk*, artistic sensibility became a significant focus. For instance, Africans did not just use iron, but they transformed it into imaginative pieces of art. They were equally creative with brass, bronze, and gold: "All the work of Benin in bronze and brass was executed by casting, and by methods so complicated that it would be no easy task for a modern European craftsman to imitate them." With all the impressive work with metals, pottery, and other items, Du Bois concluded: "Perhaps no race has shown in its earlier development a more magnificent art impulse than the Negro." To Du Bois, and he hoped to his readers as well, Africans were clearly equal or superior to European civilizations even with their different history.

These chapters on African history had huge appeal among the growing college-educated African American population. *The Negro* appeared at a time when African Americans were increasingly producing significant artistic and academic work on their past, seeking to counter the white supremacist history of race in America as well as the African past. In the same year that Du Bois published *The Negro*, Carter G. Woodson organized the Association for the Study of Negro Life and History. The thin volume seemed to open the eyes and confirm many of the ideas of a growing intellectual community. Asserting concepts that he had first proposed in "The Conservation of the Races" and again in London at the 1900 Pan-African Conference, Du Bois remarked, "Instead of being led and defended by others, as in the past, American negroes are gaining their own voices, their own ideals. Self-realization is thus coming . . . to another of the world's great races." Du Bois would take this argument even further, placing more of the Pan-African outlook in his concluding sections of *The Negro*. In a political prophecy that went beyond his proclamation on the color line in London, he wrote: "The Pan-African movement when it comes will not . . . be merely a narrow racial propaganda. Already the more far-seeing Negroes sense the coming unities: a unity of the working classes everywhere, a unity of the colored races, a new unity of men. . . . As long as black laborers are slaves, white laborers cannot be free."

The Crisis editor's focus on Africa and the international color line as the world went to war influenced his initial response to the alleged war to end all wars. In November 1914, years before America's involvement, he outlined for his readers the reasons for the war. "The present war in Europe is one of the great disasters due to race and color prejudice and it but foreshadows greater disasters in the future. It is not merely national jealousy, or the so-called 'race' rivalry of Slav, Teuton, and Latin, that is the larger cause of this war. It is rather," he explained, "the wild quest for Imperial expansion among colored races between Germany, England and France primarily, and Belgium, Italy, Russia and Austria-Hungary in a lesser degree."

Du Bois developed this argument further in his seminal essay "The African Roots of the War," published in May 1915 in *Atlantic Monthly*. In the piece, Du Bois asserted that whites throughout the world benefited from the exploitation of Africa and the nonwhite world. He outlined the detrimental history of European imperialism in Africa and how the attempts to control the continent's resources were central to understanding the origins of the conflict. According to Du Bois, greed and jealousy had driven the European nations into such frenzy that war was inevitable. In the end, according to the *Crisis* editor, the war was about Africa, and the future of modern civilization hinged on a continent free of foreign domination. The following year, he more directly argued in a *Crisis* editorial that the war was a death knell for the West. Civilization "has met its Waterloo," he declared. "We have read of attacks by gas, of raids on non-fortified towns, of Zeppelins dropping bombs on women and children, and the whole campaign of 'frightfulness' which left us at first cold and faint and even yet inspires in us a sick disaster."

Unpredictable at the time, the horrors of World War I did not destroy the West or white domination, nor did it hinder the ability to invent new ways to inflict casualties during armed conflict. While Dr. Du Bois could rightfully predict that the problem of the twentieth century was the problem of the color line—"the relation of the darker to the lighter races of men"—he could not predict the "age of extremes" that the century would travel to wrestle over the problem. Du Bois learned that the war was not the end of something old, but rather an indication of something new.

Du Bois may not have been able to predict the future, but he was the most prominent spokesperson on race in America, and the organization he was synonymous with was rapidly growing. Moreover, at nearly fifty, he had been writing, thinking, and philosophizing about issues of race, economics, education, and politics for more years than many of the current crop of race thinkers had been alive. His age did become a concern when he had to undergo surgery for kidney stones in 1916 and the removal of a kidney in 1917, a procedure that brought him "down into the valley of the shadow of death."

After Du Bois spent nearly a year recuperating, with no true break from his vigorous writing, editing, and speaking schedule, Joel Spingarn hosted a fiftieth birthday party for him at New York City's Civil Club. The event reinvigorated the doctor. He received congratulatory letters from his old Great Barrington high school principal as well as former colleagues and students. More heartening, however, may have been the birthday greetings he received from the public, his *Crisis* readers, who praised his resolve and principles and acknowledged his leadership in the fight for civil rights. As Philadelphia resident Estelle Matthews stated, she believed our country would be different if we "had a thousand brave, noble-minded men like [Du Bois]. Men who dare to speak the truth. . . . Men who can look the blue-eyed Anglo-Saxon in the face and let them know there are true hearted black men and women."

Du Bois soaked it all in. The celebration, reflection, and praise inspired the tireless "ideal leader of the Negro race," but no one knew how quickly things would change. America's involvement in the war and the issue of what to do on the domestic front would cause a number of his followers to question their support for the *Crisis* editor. For seemingly the first time, Du Bois's words and advice put him at odds with many members of the black community and as a result tarnished his reputation as a "foremost leader" of the race.

In April 1917 the United States entered the war, and many African Americans volunteered. After one failed attempt Congress passed the Selective Service Act, which provided "for the enlistment of all able-bodied Americans between the ages of twenty-one and thirty-one," on May 18, 1917. While this meant African Americans would be able to serve, the government announced that they would serve in separate units and train in segregated training camps under white officers. Such a move along with other racist policies instituted by Woodrow Wilson and his administration frustrated Du Bois. He complained to secretary of the war Newton D. Baker that the government must settle the issue because in his opinion it "interferes with winning the war." Additionally, he was enraged by the nation's silence in response to the racist riot in East St. Louis and the lynching of thirteen black soldiers following racial unrest in Houston during 1917.

Despite the anger of Du Bois, and many within the black community, about the spike in racial violence in the country and the racist policies of the Wilson administration, the majority of the NAACP members and leadership supported the war effort. The organization even supported the military's creation of segregated camps, and Joel Spingarn lobbied for Du Bois to get a "captaincy in Military Intelligence," an offer that had given Du Bois "the shock of his life. . . ." Although he was still "in principle, opposed to the war," Du Bois believed that America's involvement would become a "fight for democracy including colored folk and not merely for war investments." In addition, he imagined that any "passive resistance" by the NAACP against the war "would have fallen flat and perhaps slaughtered the American Negro body and soul."

Figure 4.1. Anti-lynching parade organized by the National Association for the Advancement of Colored People (NAACP). Ten thousand participants marched in the silent parade; women and children dressed in white and men dressed in black. Pictured from left to right in the second row: Rev. Hutchins Bishop (1); Jack Nail, prominent New York realtor (4); W. E. B. Du Bois (8); James Weldon Johnson (9). Courtesy University of Massachusetts Archives.

In the spring and summer of 1918, just a few months after his fiftieth-birthday celebration, Du Bois used the pages of *The Crisis* to give his fullest support to the war effort. The theme of the June issue was the black soldier, and in his editorial Du Bois gave his reasons for supporting the war. "This war is the End and, also, a Beginning," he stated. "Never again will darker people of the world occupy just the place they have before. Out of this war will rise, soon or late, an independent China; a self-governing India, and Egypt with representative institutions; an Africa for the Africans, and not merely for business exploitation. Out of this war," he continued, "will rise, too, an American Negro with the right to vote and the right to work and the right to live without insult. These things may not and will not come at once; but they are written in the stars, and the first step toward them is victory for the armies of the Allies."

In the next issue Du Bois took his position one step further and published a controversial editorial, "Close Ranks." He began the piece by reiterating his belief that the war was a crisis of the world and the outcome would have great consequences for Africa and the Diaspora. "We the colored race," Du Bois maintained, "have no ordinary interest in the outcome. That which the German power represents today spells death to the aspirations of Negroes and all darker races for equality, freedom and democracy." Du Bois then surprised his readers when he outlined how they could show their support for the war effort, imploring African Americans to "forget our special grievances and close our ranks shoulder to shoulder with our own white fellow citizens and the allied nations that are fighting for democracy."

Many throughout the nation could not believe that Du Bois had written these words. NAACP members in local branches debated the editorial and many criticized the man whom they had all grown to trust and follow over the past decade. Byron Gunner, a former Niagara Movement colleague and current president of William Monroe Trotter's National Equal Rights League, wrote to Du Bois that he was "unable to conceive that said advice comes from you. It seems to me that the impossible has happened and I'm amazed beyond expression." Now was "the most opportune time for us to push and keep our 'special grievances' to the fore," argued Gunner.

The growing "political new negro" crowd was also swift to question the wisdom of Du Bois's position. Chandler Owen, editor with A. Philip Randolph of the recently created *Messenger*, charged Du Bois with "supporting causes thwarting his avowed aim of integration." Later the *Messenger* editors would ask if the NAACP was "for the *advancement of colored people* or for the *advancement of certain people*." Hubert Harrison, former socialist, Garveyite, co-head of the Liberty Congress, and editor of another magazine, *The Voice*, also criticized Du Bois in a series of editorials where he argued that Du Bois's position signified "collapse of his leadership."

Harrison did not pull any punches in the devastating critique, "The Descent of Dr. Du Bois," in his 1920 book *When Africa Awakes*. Harrison recognized that Du Bois's article and new position had "a darker and more sinister significance," since it was written while the doctor was "being preened" for a position in military intelligence. According to Harrison, for these circumstances "Du Bois is regarded much in the same way as a knight in the middle ages who had his armor stripped from him, his arms reversed and his spurs hacked off. This ruins him as an influential person among

Negroes at this time, alike whether he becomes a captain or remains an editor."

Du Bois was quick to try to clarify his thinking. A month after the appearance of "Close Ranks" he wrote, "This is our country: We have worked for it, we have suffered for it, we have fought for it." He acknowledged America was not perfect, "but it has not sinned as Germany has sinned." African Americans, he asserted, must not "bargain with our loyalty" or gain profit "with our country's blood." The sacrifice and valor of black soldiers, he hoped, would "show the world again what the loyalty and bravery of black men means."

Throughout the war Du Bois stood steadfast. He would later pen "*first* your Country, *then* your Rights!" More sternly, Du Bois wrote: "By the God of Heaven, we are cowards and jackasses if now that the war is over, we do not marshal every ounce of our brain and brawn to fight a sterner, longer, more unbending battle against the forces of hell in our own land." Du Bois became increasingly disillusioned as the end of the war brought a return of bloodshed to the American landscape in unprecedented amounts; lynchings and race riots soared during what NAACP field secretary James Weldon Johnson called the "Red Summer."

During the war the industrial cities of the North and the Midwest recruited southern black workers. By 1919 an estimated 500,000 African Americans had emigrated to the North, hoping to escape the Jim Crow South and the poor rural economy. Many African Americans were hired for positions in the expanding wartime economy, and some were hired as strikebreakers. After the war, competition for jobs and the unemployment rate rose as the military rapidly demobilized with few to no plans for absorbing the returning soldiers, white and black, into the job market. Additionally, the postwar years witnessed intensifying racist portrayals of blacks in the popular media, highlighted by the prewar success of the film *The Birth of a Nation*, the postwar creation of the popular radio show *Amos 'n' Andy*, the resurgence of white supremacist groups like the Ku Klux Klan, and the spread of residential segregation.

In this environment social tensions boiled over, and in the summer and fall of 1919 race riots exploded in a number of cities in the North and the South. Three of the most violent occurred in Chicago; Washington, D.C.; and Elaine, Arkansas. In a period of nearly eight months, fourteen blacks were burned in public by white mobs, more than sixty were lynched, and more than two dozen major race riots erupted. Eminent African American historian, founder of the Association for the Study of Negro Life and History, and creator of Negro History Week (ultimately expanded and named Black History Month) Carter G. Woodson later described one scene in the nation's capital, as well as his own close call with death:

> They had caught a Negro and deliberately held him as one would a beef for slaughter, and when they had conveniently adjusted him for lynching they shot him. I heard him groaning in his struggle as I hurried away as fast as I could without running, expecting every moment to be lynched myself.

In addition to witnessing violence, African Americans experienced other frustrations. The NAACP gained hard-fought victories in *Guinn v. U.S.* (1917) and *Buchanan v. Worley* (1917), which, respectively, attacked Oklahoma's "grandfather clause" and residential segregation in a number of southern cities, but they could not gain a foothold economically as labor unions and employers continued to discriminate, as did the army and other departments of the federal government. Moreover, the armistice did not lead to the end of "white imperialism" or the rise of self-determination for the darker peoples of the world. With these postwar realities setting in, Du Bois's idealism and optimism waned, and disillusionment soared.

Twenty years later Du Bois still wrestled with his wartime stance. "I am less sure now than then," he would state in *Dusk of Dawn*, "of the soundness of this war attitude. I did not realize the full horror of war and its wide impotence as a method of social reform. Perhaps, despite words, I was thinking narrowly of the interest of my group and was willing to let the world go to hell, if the black man went free. Today I do not know; and I doubt if the triumph of Germany in 1918 could have had worse results than the triumph of the Allies. Possibly passive resistance," he argued, "of my twelve million to any war activity might have saved the world for black and white. Almost certainly such a proposal on my part would have fallen flat and perhaps slaughtered the American Negro body and soul. I do not know. I am puzzled," he admitted.

What is certain is that with the end of the war Du Bois's anger and despair escalated and his expectations were smashed, with blood running in the streets of black American communities. His discouragement was evident in a story he wrote for the *Brownies' Book*, a children's magazine he edited: "Fools, yes that's it. Fools. All of us fools fought a long, cruel, bloody and unnecessary war and we not only killed our boys—we killed Faith and

Hope." Du Bois's rage was obvious in *The Crisis* when his words screamed from the pages:

We return.
We return from fighting.
We return fighting.
Make way for Democracy! We saved it in France, and by the Great Jehovah, we will save it in the United States of America, or know the reason why.

Shortly after the closing of the war Du Bois sailed to France to represent the NAACP at the Versailles Peace Conference. As Du Bois had stated numerous times, the outcome of the conflict would have enormous consequences for Africans throughout the world, and he was present to make sure that the peace agreement would not be created as a detriment to Africans on the continent and in the Diaspora, those Africans dispersed throughout the world. Du Bois also decided that the momentous peace meetings at Versailles would be an opportune occasion to call together individuals in a Pan-African Congress so that some attention might be placed on the issues of Africans throughout the world. As Du Bois explained, to white and black Americans, the purpose of the congress was not a call for racial separatism. To him, the call for massive African emigration was "absurd." What the movement meant, he argued, was equivalent to what the "Zionist movement must mean to the Jews, the centralization of race effort and the recognition of a racial fount." Moreover, to those who saw the congress as unnecessary, Du Bois responded in a May 1919 *Crisis* editorial:

> The destinies of mankind for a hundred years to come are being settled today in a small room of the Hotel Crillon by four unobtrusive gentlemen who glance out speculatively now and then to Cleopatra's Needle on the Place de la Concorde.
>
> You need not believe this if you do not want to. They do not care what you believe. They have the POWER. They are settling the world's problems and you can believe what you choose as long as they control ARMIES and NAVIES, the world supply of CAPITAL and the PRESS.

For this reason, he argued, it was imperative that blacks had a presence and a voice in Paris along with other nationalities and organizations.

Pan-Africanism, though not new for leaders in the Diaspora or for Du Bois, became one of his principal undertakings in the 1920s. After the 1919 congress Du Bois became deeply involved in Pan-African Congresses in 1921, 1923, and 1927. In late 1923 Du Bois also made his first visit to Africa, which he said was the "greatest" event of his life. According to Du Bois, the crucial question was "whether Negroes are to lead in the rise of Africa or whether they must always and everywhere follow the guidance of white folk." While the Pan-African Congresses were not altogether successful, they did set the precedent of bringing together Diasporic voices to discuss the plight of "darker peoples of the world" and laid planks in the foundation for the ultimate independence movements in Africa, the Caribbean, and South and Central America.

Some African Americans disagreed with Du Bois's focus on the continent of Africa and the Diaspora. *Messenger* coeditor Chandler Owen asked, "Why 'democracy in Africa' alone? Why not 'American democracy' too?" Roy Wilkins, a *Kansas City Call* reporter and future Du Bois colleague in the national office of the NAACP, believed that Du Bois was "gallivanting over the country from the Atlantic to the Pacific talking Pan-Africanism when he should have been using his talents to aid degraded America." Another editor complained that Du Bois was putting much time, ink, and energy into the colonies and had failed to say a word about "his own suffering people."

While these critiques were frustrating to Du Bois, they were minuscule compared to the criticism and conflict his activities would cause between him and Marcus Garvey's Universal Negro Improvement Association

Figure 4.2.   Group portrait of delegates to the second Pan-African Congress in Belgium. Courtesy University of Massachusetts Archives.

(UNIA). Born in Jamaica in 1887, Garvey traveled to the United States in 1916 and set up the headquarters of his organization in Harlem the following year. The tumultuous upheaval of the war and its bloody aftermath in America catapulted Garvey into international prominence. Garvey's charismatic appeals to Black Nationalism, Pan-Africanism, and racial pride offered an alternative to the NAACP and attracted thousands of followers. Within a brief period of time the UNIA initiated the Black Star steamship line, the Universal African Legion, and the *Negro World* newspaper. At its height the UNIA had branches throughout the world, but its greatest success was in North America, which had more than 700 official branches by the early 1920s. The organization claimed 35,000 dues-paying members in New York City alone. Worldwide the organization claimed over two million followers, though Wilfred Adolphus Domingo, a Jamaican Garveyite who was a close confidant of the UNIA leader, counted "only" 100,000 as dues-paying members. Notwithstanding, whether its supporters were paying members or self-proclaimed Garveyites, Garvey's UNIA was a charismatic, dramatic, populist movement that spread across the United States and the world like the rising sun. As E. Franklin Frazier astutely observed in 1926, the NAACP, "which has fought uncompromisingly for equality for the Negro, has never secured, except locally and occasionally, the support of the masses. It has lacked the dramatic element." Garvey's brilliance was the ability to make "the Negro an important person in his immediate environment." This meteoritic rise of Garvey and Garveyism set the stage for a clash between the UNIA leader and all other African American leaders and organizations clamoring for the support of the black community for their individual ideas, programs, and financial adventures.

Du Bois and Garvey first met when the *Crisis* editor traveled to Jamaica in April 1915. When Garvey came to America, he had some contact with the NAACP executive, and Du Bois advertised Garvey's fund-raising activities in May 1916. At the end of the war, however, Garvey began to criticize Du Bois. Garvey sniped that Du Bois was able to go to Paris for the peace conference because he was the puppet of the white-controlled U.S. government. The following year, when Du Bois attended the UNIA's massive August convention, Garvey attacked him from the stage. "We believe Negroes are big, not by the size of their pocketbook, not by the alien company they keep, but their being for their race," he said. "You cannot advocate 'close ranks' today and talk 'dark water' tomorrow; you must be a hundred percent Negro."

Garvey's attacks of Du Bois and the NAACP would only increase. Tied to the criticism were Garvey's Jamaican-formed ideas of race and colorism. In Jamaica a different form of racial discrimination had formed, one built on a color caste system. Lighter-skinned blacks were more accepted, possessed greater economic standing, and did not experience as much discrimination as the darker Afro-Jamaican population. When he relocated to the United States, Garvey brought with him an abhorrence for any idea of race stratification in the form of light-skin privilege. These ideas were reinforced when he traveled around the country and noticed, in his estimation, that light-skinned blacks held better positions of employment and also separated themselves in some respects from darker-skinned African Americans. Garvey was even more stunned, or "dumbfounded," as he later explained, when he visited the NAACP headquarters in 1916 and found that "the whole staff was either white or very near white." Before long Garvey was referring to the NAACP as the "National Association for the Advancement of (Certain) Colored People." But it was not until his return from a fund-raising expedition in the West Indies and Central America in mid-1921, after he found himself temporarily barred from reentry into the United States, that Garvey expanded upon his ideas of race to embrace the concept of "race purity." This not only aligned him politically with groups like the Ku Klux Klan but also carried with it an implicit condemnation of the claimed social superiority of light-skinned blacks.

The UNIA president now averred that Du Bois was the evil genius, "the most dangerous of the Mulattoes," behind "that vicious Negro-hating organization known as the NAACP," a group that was "as great Negro haters as the Southern crackers are, for the simple reason [that] their program is race assimilation which will in another hundred years wipe out this Negro race and make a new race which will not be Negro in any degree." Garvey argued that Du Bois, in order to solve the race problem, was urging blacks to "commit [race] suicide by jumping over the white fence." He sought, the UNIA leader asserted, "a destruction of the black and white races by the social amalgamation of both."

The difference was not only the interracialism of the NAACP's approach, but also the perceived audience of the two leaders' messages. As one Garveyite stated, "The NAACP appeals to the Beau Brummel, Lord Chesterfield, kid-gloved, silk stocking, creased-trousered, patent leather shoe . . . element, while the UNIA appeals to the . . . hard-working man . . . [Du Bois] appeals to the 'talented tenth' while Garvey appeals to the Hoi Polloi."

Du Bois did not immediately respond to Garvey's criticisms and attacks, and when he did, he used much restraint and unanimity. In the final issue of 1920 and the first issue of 1921 of *The Crisis* he published a two-part essay on Garveyism, a movement that he judged "one of the most interesting spiritual movements of the modern Negro world." He saw Garvey as an "extraordinary leader of men" whose basic economic strategy was "perfectly feasible." "What he is trying to say and do," Du Bois explained, involves the idea that "American Negroes can, by accumulating and ministering their own capital, organize industry, join the black centers of the south Atlantic by commercial enterprise and in this way ultimately redeem Africa as a fit and free home for black men." "This is true," Du Bois declared. Garvey described Du Bois's articles as "75 percent criticism and 25 percent appreciation."

Over the next couple of years Garvey continued to attack the NAACP and Du Bois, and the professor continued to see his Pan-African endeavors increasingly misperceived by many within the black community as those of the Jamaican leader's activities. Finally, in 1923, after Garvey had been arrested and was awaiting trial for mail fraud, Du Bois unleashed his anger in an article in *Century* magazine. Du Bois launched his condemnation with a venomous attack: "A little, fat black man, ugly, but with intelligent eyes and big head," he seethed, "was seated on a plank platform beside a 'throne,' dressed in a military uniform of the gayest mid-Victorian type. . . . A casual observer might have mistaken it for the dress-rehearsal of a new comic opera. . . . But it was not; it was a serious occasion, done on the whole soberly and solemnly." Du Bois's invective assault continued: "Some Negroes would have said that this ceremony had something symbolic, like the coronation, because it was part of a great 'back-to-Africa' movement and represented self-determination for the Negro race and a relieving of America of her most difficult race problem by a voluntary operation. On the other hand, many American Negroes and some others were scandalized by something which they could but regard as simply child's play. It seemed to them sinister, this enthroning of a demagogue, a blatant boaster, who with monkey-shines was deluding the people and taking their hard-earned dollars; and in High Harlem there rose an insistent cry, 'Garvey must go!'"

Du Bois, like many in the African American community, had shifted his position on Garvey. In two short years he had moved from seeing the Jamaican leader as making an important contribution to addressing the race issue in America to concluding his critique of Garvey and Garveyism by saying that following Garvey's ideas would result in world war and eternal hate and blood. According to Du Bois, Garvey's philosophy and actions would "set the world clock back a thousand years."

Shortly after Du Bois attacked Garvey in the pages of *The Crisis* the UNIA leader was convicted of mail fraud and sent to federal prison. With Garvey's conviction came Du Bois's harshest criticism, proclaiming that the "provisional president of Africa" was "either a lunatic or a traitor." He criticized the UNIA leader for taking the hard-earned money of African Americans, conceding on the issue of black rights, and lashing out at his critics. It was "time to tell the truth about black traitors," he declared. "Garvey is, without doubt, the most dangerous enemy of the Negro race in America."

Garvey was released from federal prison in 1928. Upon his release he faced imminent deportation for his conviction and his organization was weakened by his absense during his prison stint. At this time Du Bois published a much more conciliatory comment about the UNIA leader. "He has a great and worthy dream," Du Bois stated. "He is free; he has a following; he still has a chance to carry on his work in his own home and among his own people and to accomplish some of his ideals. Let him do it," he declared. "We will be the first to applaud any success that he may have." Over time Du Bois became even more generous. In *Dusk of Dawn*, a year before Garvey's death, he acknowledged that Garvey had been "an astonishing popular leader" who had influence throughout the Western Hemisphere and in "every corner of Africa." He would later state that the UNIA "was a mass movement that could not be ignored."

Du Bois's opinions may have moderated over time, and Garvey's arrest and the eventual weakening of his influence made the tempering possible. Make no mistake, however: Du Bois believed that Garvey and Garveyism were the wrong path to address racial issues in the United States. He later stated that African Americans of the late nineteenth and early twentieth centuries had two grave temptations. "The greater one, fathered by Booker T. Washington, . . . said, 'Let politics alone, keep in your place, work hard, and do not complain.'" "The lesser, fathered by Marcus Garvey, said, 'Give up! Surrender! The struggle is useless; back to Africa and fight the white world.'" Du Bois and the NAACP were building a particular movement for the struggle for civil rights in America, and in his eyes "American Negroes stood the test well." In his estimation the majority of black Americans were supporting the NAACP's focus on interracial cooperation and legal agitation in the strugle and the discrimination, disenfranchisement, and racial violence. During the 1920s, in addition to his tussle with Garvey, Du Bois and his *Crisis* became major voices and supporters for what has become known as the Harlem Renaissance—an "artistic and sociological" movement among artists, novelists, poets, musicians, and intellectuals that reverberated through many American urban centers and became an important landmark in African American—and American—cultural history. *The Crisis* had always been, in part, a literary magazine. Du Bois had continuously given space to prose, poetry, and artistic expression. During the first decade William Stanley Braithwaite edited the poetry selections, but in 1919 Du Bois hired Jessie Redmond Fauset to edit the magazine's literature. Fauset and Du Bois published many young writers, including Claude McKay, Langston Hughes, Gwendolyn Brooks, Arna Bontemps, and Zora Neale Hurston. Hughes recalled that *The Crisis* "mid-wifed the so-called Negro literature into being."

With *The Crisis*, Fauset, Walter White, James Weldon Johnson, Du Bois, and the NAACP were at the center of the artistic movement; they not only published their own work, they also provided mentoring and support to other artists and thinkers of the renaissance. The organization gave literary prizes for outstanding books, and in 1928 Du Bois's daughter Yolanda Du Bois married the incredibly talented poet Countee Cullen. Though the marriage only lasted a short period, the wedding itself was a cultural and social event, with fifteen hundred guests in attendance.

During the period Du Bois attempted to provide a cultural philosophy for the New Negro in literature. In the June 1921 issue of *The Crisis* the editor observed that too many African Americans "want everything that is said about us to tell of the best and highest and noblest in us. We need to insist that our Art and Propaganda must be one. This is wrong and in the end it is harmful." The editor encouraged writers to "face the Truth of Art. We have criminals and prostitutes, ignorant and debased elements, just as all folk have. . . . The black Shakespeare must portray his black Iagos as well as his white Othellos." A little later he explained, "The great mission of the Negro to America is the development of Art and the appreciation of Beauty." Artists, he argued, needed to ground their works in the diversity of the black experience, "our love of life, the world and beautiful desire of our women and men for each other."

Within a few years, however, Du Bois would become increasingly frustrated by the style and content of many of the products of the renaissance. He did not agree with Charles S. Johnson, a sociologist and editor of the Urban League's *Opportunity* magazine, that artistic products could substitute for agitation, petitions, and marches on behalf of social justice. Or as historian David Levering Lewis has put it, the New Negro might pursue "Civil Rights through copyright."

The doctor's frustration with many artists' emphasis on art as an instrument for changing the material and political realities of black life led him to once again try to assert his own philosophy on the movement. At the 1926 national conference of the NAACP, Du Bois delivered a serious critique of the aesthetic positions of many of the renaissance artists. "Do we want simply to be Americans?" he asked the audience. "We who are dark can see America in a way that white Americans can not. . . . Thus, are we satisfied with its present goals or ideals?" His answer was no. The "apostle of Beauty," he argued, must also be bound to the "apostle of Truth and Right," if the goals of black freedom were to be served. "Thus all Art is propaganda and ever must be, despite the wailing of the pursuits." "I do not care a damn," he declared, "for any art that is not used for propaganda."

He also began to criticize writers who fell into their own stereotypical trappings and only portrayed Harlem as a place of cabarets and sin. Of particular frustration were works like Carl Van Vechten's *Nigger Heaven* (1926), Julia Peterkin's *Black April* (1927), and Claude McKay's *Home to Harlem* (1928). McKay's novel was the first by a black writer to become a best seller, but Du Bois was frustrated because the book focused on "the debauched Tenth," "drunkenness, fighting, lascivious sexual promiscuity and utter absence of restraint." He claimed that the book left him feeling nauseated and that "after the dirtier parts of its filth" he felt "like taking a bath."

Before, during, and after the renaissance Du Bois continued to publish creative and scholarly work alongside his material in *The Crisis*. In 1911 he released his first novel, *The Quest of the Silver Fleece*. The novel, arguably his best, is a sentimental, romantic tale about Blessed Alwyn and Zora, but underneath the romance the book is a study of the "moral and political consequences" of African American life in post-Reconstruction America. Du Bois, like other artists of the period, including Paul Laurence Dunbar, Charles Chesnutt, T. Thomas Fortune, and others, were using literature to counter the narrative of the postemancipation era being presented to the nation in the works of invididuals such as Joel Chandler Harris and Thomas Dixon. In the end, according to Du Bois, *The Quest of the Silver Fleece* was "an economic study of some merit."

At the end of the war he published *Darkwater: Voices from within the Veil* (1920), a collection of essays similar to those of *The Souls of Black Folk*. Additionally, *Darkwater* involved the same shifting styles from exposition and polemic to poetry and allegory, and it contained historical and sociological discourses on education, race, economics, and politics. Four years later he published *The Gift of Black Folk: Negroes in the Making of America* (1924) as part of a series that was intended "as a much needed and important contribution to national solidarity." *The Gift of Black Folk* fits the objectives of the series; it not only traces the effect that "the Negro has had upon American life," but also the spiritual "gifts" African Americans have contributed to the nation and "civilization." Du Bois uses these "gifts" as a way to critique white American society and demonstrate how African Americans have kept the "truer souls," a moral path, as the nation has increasingly become a "materialistic, philistine, aggressive culture."

During the renaissance Du Bois also published his second novel, *Dark Princess: A Romance* (1928). Similar to *The Quest for the Silver Fleece*, at its heart the book is a romance novel, but unlike his first novel, which was set in the United States, *Dark Princess* takes place outside America and focuses on an international organization of the "darker peoples of the world." Du Bois, who once called it "my favorite book," characterized the story as "a story of the great movement of the darker races for self-expression and self-determination." In the story the darker races unite under an Indian princess to fight against European domination. *Dark Princess* was Du Bois's attempt to put his ideas of "art as propaganda" into practice, an attempt to exemplify what he meant by politically effective art.

By the time of the NAACP's twentieth anniversary the association had become the county's most influential civil rights organization. The association had built more than 320 branches throughout the country and had a membership whose dues paid the vast majority of the national office's $55,000 yearly operating budget. Moreover, Du Bois, predominantly through his work in editing *The Crisis*, had regained his position as the nation's most prominent spokesman for black Americans on the eve of the Depression. He had prevailed over Booker T. Washington and outlasted Garvey, who had been deported; survived his poorly received wartime "close ranks" comment; and, with the assistance of other NAACP members, had navigated the race through the postwar period and the cultural awakening of the Harlem Renaissance. The next decade would not prove to be as promising for Du Bois. New

NAACP leadership and the economic downturn of the nation had deleterious effects on the association and its best-known leader.

Chapter Five

The Wings of Atlanta and the NAACP Redux

This the American black man knows: his fight here is a fight to the finish. Either he dies or wins. If he wins it will be by no subterfuge or evasion of amalgamation. He will enter modern civilization here in America as a black man on terms of perfect and unlimited equality with any white man, or he will enter not at all. Either extermination root and branch, or absolute equality. There can be no compromise. This is the last great battle of the West.

—W. E. B. Du Bois, 1935

During his time with the NAACP and *The Crisis* Du Bois became more doubtful about the effectiveness of his preferred approach to end America's racial disparities, and over the course of the 1920s he began to shift or alter previously held positions. For instance, in earlier years he implored African Americans not to consent to the development of separate schools, but in the 1920s he questioned that steadfast position and began to criticize integrated school systems where black students were "abused, browbeaten, murdered, and kept in something worse than ignorance." His shift began to expand, as he believed the only progress that had been made in recent years was the development and growth of all-black activities and institutions. "There seems no hope," he pessimistically explained, that the white American "in our day will yield in its color or race hatred any substantial ground and we have not physical nor economic power, nor any alliance with other social or economic classes that will force compliance with decent civilized ideals in Church, State, industry, or art." He also suggested that African Americans look in-ward with his promotion of cooperatives, or a closed black "economic circle." In August of 1918 he held a meeting at *The Crisis* to establish the Negro Cooperative Guild. "The whole movement" failed, however, because African Americans lacked "popular education as both consumers and managers."

During the 1930s, as the devastating consequences of the Depression were taking their toll on the black community, he again looked internally for solutions and solace. "In a world where economic dislocation had become so great as in ours," he wrote, "a mere appeal based on the old liberalism, a mere appeal to justice . . . was missing the essential need," which was "to guard and better the chances of Negroes, educated and ignorant, to earn a living, safeguard their income, and raise the level of their employment." If African Americans were going to be saved, Du Bois saw no real approach at the time but to look to themselves.

> Instead of our sitting like dumb and patient fools awaiting the salvation of the white industrial Lord, it is our duty now to prepare for a new organization and a new status, new modes of making a living, and a new organization of industry.
>
> If we expect to enter present or future industry upon our own terms, we must have terms; we must have power; we must learn the secret of economic organization; we must submit to leadership, not of words but of ideas; we must weld the civilized part of these 12 million of our race into an industrial phalanx that cannot be ignored, and which Americans and the world will come to regard as a strong asset under any system and not merely as a weak and despicable liability.

In 1933 at Fisk University, where Du Bois delivered a commencement address, he further developed his argument. "We have not assurance this twentieth century civilization will survive. We do not know that American Negroes will survive," he told the graduates. "There are sinister signs about us, antecedent to and unconnected with the Great Depression. The organized might of industry north and south is relegating the Negro to the edge of survival and using him as a labor reservoir on starvation wage." Du Bois returned to the idea of a separate economy and the idea of "self-segregation," a decision that was not reached "by choice but by force."

> You do not get humanity by wishing it nor do you become American citizens simply because you want to. A Negro university . . . does not advocate segregation by race; it simply accepts the bald fact that we are segregated, apart, hammered into a separate unity by spiritual intolerance and legal sanction backed by mob law, and that this separation is growing in strength and fixa-

tion . . . and that no character, address, culture or desert is going to change it in our day or for centuries to come. . . . We are segregated; we are a caste. This is our given and at present unalterable fact. Our problem is: How far and in what way can we consciously and scientifically guide our future so as to insure our physical survival, our spiritual freedom and our social growth? Either we do this or we die.

During this period Du Bois also became increasingly isolated within the NAACP. He stayed close to Joel Spingarn, the chairman of the board, but his relationship with executive secretary Walter White deteriorated year by year. According to Du Bois, when White first joined the organization and worked as James Weldon Johnson's assistant, he got along well with his coworkers. He placed himself in harm's way investigating lynchings, as he was light enough to pass for white. He was a team player and carried out Johnson's plans with "a ready smile" and "a sense of humor." By the late 1920s, however, White's collegial work ethic deteriorated and in doing so made

Figure 5.1. Group portrait of W. E. B. Du Bois, his wife Nina, and James Weldon Johnson standing in front of the Burghardt family homestead in Great Barrington, Massachusetts. Courtesy University of Massachusetts Archives.

Johnson's job more difficult. Johnson told Du Bois that if things continued to worsen, he would have to resign. Du Bois believed White thought he should be the organization's chief executive "instead of working under Johnson."

Johnson's resignation came in 1931 when he decided to become writer-in-residence at Fisk University, and Du Bois's prognostication proved correct: White was the chosen successor. White proved to be an unpopular choice to helm the nation's premier civil rights organization, and employees began leaving the main office nearly immediately. Mary White Ovington, who was the chairman of the board of directors, summed up the feelings of many when she resigned. She explained to Joel Spingarn that White rarely consulted with her and often failed to include her in meetings. She later characterized him as "a dictator" who squashed discussion and opposition and pushed the board into taking a "rubber stamp attitude." White increased the frustration in New York when he criticized field secretary William Pickens and director of branches Robert W. Bagnall, long-standing NAACP members, for failing to raise sufficient funds for the organization. He then recommended the release of twelve-year veteran Pickens and the reassignment of Bagnall. Du Bois led an unsuccessful revolt against White and his leadership of the organization. After this, White mended his ways and pulled many of the board back to his side for the time being.

Du Bois was not easily swayed by White's new attitude. He had no confidence in the new chief executive or Roy Wilkins, his assistant secretary. In 1931 Du Bois told Joel Spingarn that he would leave *The Crisis* and the organization if the board did not limit White's power. The frustrated but seasoned activist later complained that he would not work with an editorial board that was not limited if White sat on the board. He added the same for Wilkins, who, he told Spingarn, was White's "errand boy." He also told board member Lillian Alexander that he was "getting terribly tired fooling away time and energy on Walter White. He is neither straight nor honest." Du Bois believed the executive's "attitudes and actions were unbearable," and the NAACP, which had formerly been a "nursery of ideas," was turning into an unenlightened corporation.

After White's ascendency to power in the NAACP, Du Bois found that his difficulties with White and his leadership went beyond personality conflicts. As the economy struggled in the early 1930s, both the organization and *The Crisis* became cash-strapped, but the head office contributed funds to keep the magazine afloat. On the eve of his resignation, James Weldon Johnson had stated that "*The Crisis* is a better magazine today than it ever was," but because of the desperate economic times, many African Americans could no longer afford a subscription. By 1932 monthly circulation had fallen to about 15,000, and the magazine could not continue unless the organization paid his salary and provided additional production funds. Seeing an opportunity, White pushed for more oversight of *The Crisis*, but Du Bois threatened to resign in order to maintain control.

White's malicious maneuvering only increased as Du Bois continued to more openly pronounce a break with the NAACP's form of liberalism and reform. "In a world where economic dislocation had become so great as ours," Du Bois wrote, "a mere appeal based on the old liberalism, a mere appeal to justice . . . was missing the essential need," which was "to guard and better the chances of Negroes, educated and ignorant, to earn a living, safe-guard their income, and raise the level of their employment." With these words Du Bois moved outside the vast majority of the NAACP's comfort zone, yet he persisted in trumpeting the virtues of "self-segregation" and the "closed economic circle."

Much of Du Bois's position, however, was not new; he had been discussing variations of his "nation within a nation" idea for a number of years with little to no backlash from the NAACP or the black community. In 1919, for instance, he wrote an essay on "Jim Crow" in *The Crisis* arguing that "much of the objection to segregation and Jim Crowism was in other days the fact that compelling Negroes to associate only with Negroes meant to exclude them from contact with the best culture of the day." But he believed that times had changed and "culture was no longer the monopoly of the white" community. "The real battle," he argued, "is a matter of study and thought; of the building of loyalties; of the long training of men; of the growth of institutions; of the inculcation of racial and national ideals." African Americans should not give up all separate efforts in schools, churches, institutions, or associations.

He made a similar pragmatic decision a few years later when he supported the retention of Cheyney State Normal School, located outside of Philadelphia, as an all-black school. He was clear that while he opposed segregation in principle, he believed that one had to fight to improve whatever institution was segregated. Thus, he and the community, in his opinion, were faced with a paradox: "we must oppose segregation in schools; we must honor and appreciate the colored teacher in the colored school. . . . We recognize one thing worse than segregation," he argued, "and that is ignorance." He further maintained that often the effort for integration was a means to make or keep African Americans subordinate. According to Du Bois, the so-called integrated schools did not support black students. Integrated schools did not have the best interests of the black pupils in mind; there was little to no inspiration or encouragement. Instead, he argued, the school officials often abused, browbeat, or even murdered the students in an integrated environment. This, according to the doctor, left African American students in a state of ignorance, and "Negro children must not be allowed to grow up in ignorance. This is worse than segregation, worse than anything we could contemplate."

Over a decade later Du Bois would again support the idea of selective segregation. In the January 1934 issue of *The Crisis* he set forth his position. "The thinking colored people of the United States must stop being stampeded by the word segregation," he stated. Opposition to segregation should not "be any distaste or unwillingness of colored people to work with each other, to cooperate with each other, to live with each other." Rather, he argued, opposition to segregation should be a stance against discrimination. Moreover, according to Du Bois, segregation and discrimination "do not necessarily go together, and there should never be an opposition to segregation pure and simple unless that segregation does involve discrimination." He also reminded his readers "that in the last quarter of a century, the advance of the colored people has been mainly in the lines where they themselves, working by and for themselves, have accomplished the greatest advance." Therefore, he encouraged the black community to consider turning inward to assist themselves.

Du Bois understood that many within the black community believed that if blacks voluntarily segregated, the white community would take the opportunity to attack and bolster discrimination. He argued that the "counter attack should be against this discrimination; against the refusal of the South to spend the same amount of money on the black child as on the white child for its education; against the inability of black groups to use public capital; against the monopoly of credit by white groups. But never in the world," he argued, "should our fight be against association with ourselves because by that very token we give up the whole argument that we are worth associating with." It was, Du Bois insisted, "the race-conscious black man cooperating . . . in his own institutions and movements who will eventually emancipate the colored race."

Following the publication of this piece, Du Bois launched an offensive on segregation, explaining to *Crisis* readers that the organization had never taken a hard and fast position on fighting segregation where discrimination was involved and upholding segregation where discrimination was not involved. Over the next several months a lot of ink was spilled trying to flesh out what the organization's position was or should be on the issue of segregation. Du Bois continued to push the virtues of self-segregation and his ideas of a closed economic circle. In the April 1934 issue of *The Crisis* he argued that "the net result" of the organization's twenty-five-year "campaign against segregation . . . has been a little less than nothing." In the same issue he also mocked the leaders of the NAACP, in particular Walter White, with whom, as discussed earlier, Du Bois had become increasingly frustrated in the 1930s. The doctor seemed to let all his hostility and exasperation come out on the page when he viciously opined that White "has more white companions and friends than colored . . . , for the simple and sufficient reason that he isn't 'colored.'"

For White and many others within the NAACP, any acceptance of segregation, voluntary or forced, would undermine what they saw as the primary focus of the NAACP: the dismantling of all de jure and de facto segregation and the upholding of the Fourteenth and Fifteenth Amendments. Du Bois's editorial, however, had compelled the organization to formally consider their position on segregation, something they had never done previously.

In the May 1934 issue of *The Crisis* Du Bois published an editorial, "The Board of Directors on Segregation," in which he drafted a position on segregation for the association to adopt. Members of the organization significantly rewrote the proposal before it was put before the board for a vote. The rewritten statement took Joel Spingarn's position that a necessary evil was still evil. Moreover, it stated, "We give assurance to the white and colored peoples of the world that this organization stands where it has always stood, as the chief champion of equal rights for black and white, and as unalterably opposed to the basic principles of racial segregation." This resolution ultimately gained approval from the board after it was modified to state boldly, "Both principle and practice necessitate unyielding opposition to any and every form of enforced segregation."

This move by the board left Du Bois with few options, and on June 11, 1934, he submitted his resignation as the editor of *The Crisis* and as a member of the NAACP. The news of his resignation provoked strong statements from around the country. The influential *Chicago Defender* published photographs of Du Bois and Booker T. Washington. Over the image of Washington was the reflective headline "WAS HE RIGHT AFTER ALL?" Over Du Bois: "IS HE A QUITTER?"

With his resignation, an era in the history of the NAACP, and African American civil rights history, came to an end. For more than twenty years his words had poked and prodded the nation's consciousness. As he stated six years later in *Dusk of Dawn*:

> I think I may say without boasting that in the period from 1910 to 1930 I was a main factor in revolutionizing the attitude of the American Negro toward caste. My stinging hammer blows made Negroes aware of themselves, confident of their possibilities and determined in self-assertion. So much so that today common slogans among the Negro people are taken bodily from the words of my mouth.

Du Bois's thoughts, musings, and stinging editorial pen had been organizing the black community throughout his period as editor of *The Crisis*. He was not the most radical African American intellectual, nor was he the most conservative. Moreover, as he strived to find ways to solve the nation's "racial problems," he was sometimes inconsistent and contradictory. As he stated, "I am not worried about being inconsistent. . . . What worries me is the Truth," and to find the truth, one had to be flexible and willing to adjust their perspective. This was certainly the case as he struggled with the NAACP leadership on the issue of segregation. He was searching for racial and economic justice in the United States and approached the issues from multiple fronts. This search would continue after his resignation. Though he was finishing what would be one of the most important periods of his life, the time he exercised the greatest influence within black America, he would continue to struggle, deliberately publish, and be relevant.

So at the age of sixty-six, when most people are retired or preparing for retirement, W. E. B. Du Bois returned to the life of a scholar. In 1929 a close friend, John Hope, became president of Atlanta University and extended an invitation to Du Bois to return to the university to pursue a career as an activist and propagandist. In 1933 he delivered a series of lectures at the university, and following his resignation from the NAACP, he officially returned to his academic home to lead the Department of Sociology. Over the course of his second tenure at the university, Du Bois kept a dynamic research and publication agenda. He finished projects or unpublished works, including "The Negro and Social Reconstruction" (1936) and a book-length manuscript, "The Sorcery of Color." He also published over 350 newspaper articles in addition to three other books: his seminal *Black Reconstruction*; *Black Folk Then and Now*, with a return to Africa as a research focus; and *Dusk of Dawn*, a new autobiography. Furthermore, the doctor would create a new academic journal, *Phylon*, as well as respond to a world transforming with the rise of Hitler, a world war, and the aftermath of conflict.

When Du Bois returned south, Nina stayed in New York with Yolanda, and the country was still in the midst of the Great Depression. For African Americans the Depression had started before the October 1929 stock market crash. During the 1920s, southern black farmers suffered the devastating impact of the boll weevil on their cotton harvests. They also faced a collapse in farm prices following World War I after President Woodrow Wilson lifted agricultural price supports and cut back from wartime orders.

Additionally, from the onset of World War I through World War II, one of the largest internal migrations in American history occurred when many blacks abandoned farming and moved to the cities in the South and the North. The formal onset of the Depression, however, cut the limited prosperity many of the migrants found in the urban areas. The worsening economic conditions also sharpened racial hostilities. By 1932 roughly half of the black workers in New York City, Chicago, Philadelphia, and Detroit were without jobs, and nearly one out of three African American families were receiving some form of public assistance. Moreover, the black unemployment rate greatly exceeded the white rate. For example, in Pittsburgh during 1933, 48 percent of black workers were unemployed; the comparable figure for whites was 31 percent. Lynchings of African Americans also rose, from seven in 1929 to twenty in 1930, and to twenty-four in 1933, the worst year of the economic collapse.

The devastating impact of the Depression on the black community and race relations pushed Du Bois and many other black scholars and activists to adjust their thinking and alter their programs in the 1930s. The NAACP had no effective program to attack black unemployment or the rising rates of homelessness and hunger throughout the Depression-stricken community. During this period the Marxist left and activist black members of the Communist Party, such as economist Abram L. Harris, Communist Party activists and labor organizers Angelo Herndon and Hosea Hudson, became a social force. Along with others, they created an alternative radical movement, opening new avenues of protest and ways to discuss important political issues affecting their communities. The left helped to organize a series of protest associations involving African Americans, including tenants' rights groups, sharecroppers' unions, and the Southern Negro Youth Conference.

As mentioned earlier, Du Bois was exposed to socialism while studying in Germany, where he attended meetings of the German Social Democratic Party. He remained interested in socialist ideals throughout the first couple of decades of the twentieth century. In 1907, from the pages of *The Horizon*, he wrote favorably about socialists and soon afterward joined the Socialist Party, which had been organized in 1901 and was led by Eugene Debs. A few years later, however, he left the party, criticizing it for racism, and endorsed Woodrow Wilson for president.

In the 1920s and 1930s Du Bois began to read more Karl Marx; investigated the progress of the Soviet Union, a country that he first traveled to in 1926; and shifted his belief that specific economic programs to assist the masses were more important than a total investment in social equality. For Du Bois African Americans needed to look neither to Communism nor to socialism; he saw the former as "dogmatic" and "invalid" and preferred "economic organization within the Negro group." The adjustment to his thinking led him to call for separate economic and social alignments in which African Americans would plot their own courses toward self-sufficiency. This ultimately led to his resignation from the NAACP but also expanded how he thought and wrote about the African American past, present, and future.

As literary and cultural scholar William E. Cain has argued, Du Bois's emphasis in the 1930s "on racial solidarity and economic cooperation proved momentous for his political development." It allowed him to make connections with exploited workers throughout the world and his struggle against imperialism. Whatever the differences in race, ethnic background, and religion, argued Du Bois, all workers suffered under capitalism and imperialism, and this common experience was an untapped power. In "The Negro and Social Reconstruction" (1936), written for Alain Locke's "Bronze Booklets" but unpublished until 1985, Du Bois outlined his self-determination plan and his belief in Marxism, while connecting the ideals of socialism to his economic vision for African Americans and its resonance for workers throughout the world. Du Bois declared that he was "convinced of the essential truth of the Marxian philosophy and believed that eventually land, machines and materials must belong to the state, that private profit must be abolished, that the system of exploiting labor must disappear, that people who work must have essentially equal income and that in their hands the political rulership of the state must eventually rest."

Du Bois argued for the black community to form cooperatives, an internal economy organizing their consumer power, which would launch a vanguard action against capitalism and incarnate the socialism that was destined to envelop the world and destroy imperialism, creating networks of workers worldwide. Such a move, however, would take reeducation in all forms of thought and organizing. As Du Bois explained, "Such co-operation as we have carried out within the race has been carried out in accordance with the private idea; that is, owners of capital. What I propose," argued the doctor, "is a complete revolution in that attitude; that we begin the process of training for socialism which must be done in every labor group in every country in the world, by organizing a nationwide collective system on a nonprofit basis with the ideal that the consumer is the center and the beginning of the organization; and that to him all profits over the cost of production shall be returned." According to Du Bois, such a proposal, with its worldwide aspirations, was a "far-fetched dream," but he believed it was "worth contemplation."

The first major study Du Bois finished during his second stint at Atlanta University was *Black Reconstruction: An Essay toward a History of the Part Which Black Folk Played in the Attempt to Reconstruct Democracy in America, 1860-1880* (1935). He had written on Reconstruction previously, but in the 1930s he gave the subject "continuous and concentrated" time. In 1931, while still editor of *The Crisis*, he asked the NAACP board of directors for assistance to write a history of the Reconstruction period to counter recent studies that interpreted the postwar years as a "Tragic Era," a period of misplaced "Negro rule" and disorder. He did secure support from the Rosenwald Fund to begin the project and later gained assistance from the Carnegie Corporation.

Black Reconstruction, published in 1935 after numerous revisions, including some late in the process that caused Du Bois to assume the costs, broke new ground in the fields of African American, American, and southern histories. He offered a sweeping revisionist interpretation of the role of African Americans in the Civil War and Reconstruction, as well as the national economic benefits to reunion at the expense of civil rights. The failure of Reconstruction, according to Du Bois, was "the revolutionary suppression not only of Negro suffrage but of the economic development of Negro and white labor." It was not until the 1880s that "white labor in the South" began "to realize that they had lost a great opportunity, that when they united to disfranchise the black laborer they had cut the voting power of the laboring class in two."

As historian David Levering Lewis has stated, the greatest achievement of *Black Reconstruction* "was to weave a credible historical narrative in which black people, suddenly admitted to citizenship in an environment of feral hostility, displayed admirable volition and intelligence, as well as the indolence and ignorance inherent in three centuries of bondage." Du Bois placed four million slaves at the center of the story of Reconstruction, as they seized long-overdue freedom, education, the vote, and political office. Finally, *Black Reconstruction* included an evisceration of the racist underpinnings of the day's leading historians, such as William A. Dunning and Walter Lynwood Fleming. "The whole history of Reconstruction has with few exceptions been written by passionate believers in the inferiority of the Negro. The whole body of facts concerning what the Negro actually said and did . . . is masked in such a cloud of charges, exaggeration and biased testimony, that most students . . . simply [repeat] all current legends of black buffoons in legislature, golden spittoons for fieldhands, bribery and extravagance on an unheard-of scale, and the collapse of civilization until an outraged nation rose in wrath and ended that ridiculous travesty." Du Bois's massive study of Reconstruction and his critique of the current scholarship of the period outlined the scholarly revision of the post–Civil War years over the previous fifty years, and the book remains at the center of what historian David W. Blight has called Du Bois's "struggle for American historical memory."

Even though many scholars today believe that critics attacked and dismissed *Black Reconstruction*, in fact the book initially received favorable reviews. The *New York Herald-Tribune, Literary Digest, New York American*, and *Daily Mirror* all greeted Du Bois's work enthusiastically. Jonathan Daniels, a liberal white southern newspaperman, commented in the *Book-of-the Month Club News* that *Black Reconstruction* was a correction "for much of white history about a period in which the Negro played a great part." Additionally, the black community responded favorably. Walter White put his distaste for Du Bois aside and forwarded a copy of the book to Eleanor Roosevelt, explaining to his former colleague that he "wanted her to get this more accurate picture of the Reconstruction period so that she would understand more clearly the southern scene as it is today." Finally, the impact on the community and African American social, political, and moral thought is best reflected in Illinois Department of Labor clerk Bernice Hereford's letter to Du Bois: "Is it asking too much for you to autograph one [book] for me to keep and to use as a symbol to my boys[?] To give them courage to fight on."

Black Reconstruction, in combination with the essays Du Bois wrote before and after leaving the NAACP, demonstrated his increasing skepticism about his previous integrationist philosophy. Starting in the late teens he had been adjusting his thought, writing a number of essays advocating separate education and self-segregated economic and social structures for African Americans—a "nation within a nation," as he called it. Du Bois was not becoming an advocate of nationalism, as some scholars have argued. He felt that his separatist programs were not a capitulation to racism but rather a stage in black America's development that would ultimately lead to equality.

One of the most controversial articulations of this evolving opinion was "A Negro Nation within a Nation," published in the June 1935 issue of *Current History*. Du Bois asserted that African Americans were coming to understand that "white Americans do not like them, and are planning neither for their survival, nor for their definite future if it involves free, self-assertive modern manhood." Blacks, according to Du Bois, had no choice but to organize along collective lines. "With the use of their political power, their power as consumers . . . Negroes can develop in the United States an eco-nomic nation within a nation, able to work through inner cooperation, to found its own institutions, to educate its genius, and at the same time, without mob violence or extremes of race hatred."

Many of Du Bois's contemporaries believed that Du Bois, at sixty-seven, was out of touch, contradictory, and self-defeating. In April 1935 George Streator, a young protégée of Du Bois who had joined the *Crisis* staff in 1933 but left shortly after Du Bois's resignation, informed his mentor, "There is no such thing as a separate consumer's economy." "You," he told Du Bois, "count on the Negro middle class to usher in this cooperation, but Streator urged his mentor to cease dulling his visions. After all, he urgued that Du Bois's former associates in the NAACP should have given him "ample proof" that he cannot count on "a lousy minority bourgeoisie." Du Bois replied by stating that the strategy was simply "to get Negroes thinking from a consu-mer's point of view, which is the only way to gauge their real power." He believed that black cooperativism would ultimately establish a unity between black and white workers. Streator and individuals such as E. Franklin Frazi-er, Ralph Bunche, and George S. Schuyler were unconvinced.

While back in the academic world without the demanding schedule of publishing a monthly magazine, Du Bois took the opportunity to travel, going to Germany, the Soviet Union, China, and Japan in 1936. After spending time in the Soviet Union, where he observed what he deemed as Marxist theory in action and practice, Du Bois became a keener supporter of the social and political philosophy than he had been after his previous visit to the developing Communist nation. He was interested in using more formal Marxian analysis in his work and in his writing.

In this period he also sought to revive a project he had been contemplating since the turn of the century, the *Encyclopedia of the Negro*. The encyclopedia, a projected multivolume collection with numerous contributors, was to be a statement against racism. "An editorial board under my leadership would, of course, make certain assumptions concerning Negroes" that many still think are "unproven." "These assumptions," he later stated, "would revolve around the belief that black folk are human beings, with reactions essentially the same as those of other human beings." While the encyclopedia was a worthwhile project, Du Bois could never secure funding for it. Moreover, it became a conflict between the Atlanta professor and Carter G. Woodson, who claimed that he too had planned to create an encyclopedia and charged that Du Bois was taking his idea.

The struggles to create the encyclopedia did not slow down Du Bois's productivity. He continued to work with graduate students at Atlanta, publish his newspaper columns, and generally educate the "intelligentsia" that the NAACP had credited him with creating. In 1939 that continued education led him back to Africa, and he published *Black Folk Then and Now: An Essay in the History and Sociology of the Negro Race*. Even with his impressive foresight, Du Bois could not have predicted the burgeoning African independence movement and the black freedom movement in the Americas that was soon to rise in the wake of World War II. In fact, many would have believed that white superiority and supremacy would continue to hold with a Hitler-controlled Germany gaining strength in Europe, an imperialist Great Britain, a depressed United States, and a neutral Soviet Union. In spite of the current situation, or maybe because of it, Du Bois returned to Africa to outline the glorious past of the continent and the struggles of the various groups in the African Diaspora. Reviving sections from his previous volume on Africa, *The Negro*, Du Bois again tried to draw together "into one succinct but comprehensive whole" the diverse histories of the scattered African peoples. As Du Bois explained in his introduction:

I do not for a moment doubt that my Negro descent and narrow group culture have in many cases predisposed me to interpret my facts too favorably for my race; but there is little danger of long misleading here, for the champions of white folk are legion. The Negro has long been the clown of history, the football of anthropology, and the slave of industry. I am trying to show here why these attitudes can no longer be maintained. I realize that the truth of history lies not in the mouth of partisans but rather in the calm Science that sits between. Her cause I seek to serve, and wherever I fail, I am at least paying Truth the respect of earnest effort.

Du Bois devoted chapters to Africa's ancient history and culture, the transatlantic slave trade, and the rise of the abolitionist movement. Additionally, as he explained to one friend, the book contained "enough Marx lugged

Figure 5.2.   Du Bois with Nnamdi Azikiwe, who later became governor-general of independent Nigeria. Courtesy University of Massachusetts Archives.

in to make some of my friends unhappy." Such sentiment was evident in the
sections where Du Bois examined black America's long struggle for civil
and political rights. And in his analysis he placed the black freedom movements within a global social and political context of struggles between capitalism and the workers of the world.

In 1940 Du Bois also started *Phylon: A Quarterly Review of Race and
Culture*, a social science journal. He had originally tried to create the journal
as a joint venture with Howard University's Rayford W. Logan and Charles
S. Johnson of Fisk University. Johnson later backed out of the arrangement.
Du Bois, however, wanting to make an academic journal that was equivalent
to or would rival Carter G. Woodson's *Journal of Negro History* and Charles
Thompson's *Journal of Negro Education*, both based in Washington, D.C.,
pressed forward without Johnson, stating in his first editorial that the journal
would "proceed from the point of view and the experience of the black folk
where we live and work, to the wider world." Broadly he envisioned *Phylon*
(meaning "race, stock" in Greek) as a revival of the Atlanta Studies programs
he had organized during his first tenure at the university. While *Phylon* and
the institutes connected with it did not quite live up to its editor's dreams, the
journal became a leading black social science publication. It ceased publication in 2002, nearly forty years after Du Bois's death.

In the same year that Du Bois issued the first edition of *Phylon* he also
published *Dusk of Dawn: An Essay Toward an Autobiography of a Race
Concept* (1940), an unconventional autobiography that mixed memoir and
sociological commentary. David Levering Lewis notes that, with *Dusk of
Dawn*, Du Bois "intended to write not so much the story of his own life . . .
but the autobiography of the twentieth century as it had lived through him—
'the autobiography of a concept of race,' he explained, 'elucidated and mag-
nified and doubtless distorted in the thoughts and deeds which were mine. . . .
Thus for all time my life is significant for all lives of men.'"

The book has three overall parts. The first four chapters, less than one-
third of the work, are autobiographical. The next section is a series of chapters on the concept of race and its impact on American society. Du Bois
presents race as a social construct, not a biological certainty. Refuting the
scientific definition of race of his day, he argues that their common history; a
social heritage of slavery; and discrimination, not genetics, unite people of
color. European colonizers and American segregationists have used their
idea of "race" to control, dominate, and alter the lives of black folk. The last
two chapters return the author to autobiography, recalling his life from the

creation of *The Crisis* and provide commentary on current national and international developments.

In the pages of *Dusk of Dawn* Du Bois expounds upon three key beliefs or political issues he had been ruminating on and discussing over the past few years. First, he again promotes and defends his theory that voluntary self-segregation is the best current option for advancing African Americans in their social, political, and economic struggle in the United States. In 1940 African Americans were still suffering greatly from the effects of the Depression; Du Bois saw a "segregated economy" as the only solution. He is quick to attempt to silence his critics by denying that he advocates "nationalism among Negroes." "Self-segregation" to him is a tactical maneuver "to obtain admission of the colored group to cooperation and incorporation into the white group on the best possible terms." He assures his readers that the "ultimate objective" is "full Negro rights and Negro equality in America."

Secondly, he attempts to make clear his present stance on Communism. "I was not and am not a communist," he argues; "I do not believe in the dogma of inevitable revolution in order to right economic wrong. I think war is worse than hell, and that it seldom or never forwards the advance of the world." Nevertheless, Marxism was correct in emphasizing the economic foundations of culture, "and this conviction I had to express or spiritually die." Finally, he sees the rise of Hitler and Nazi Germany, the country where he found refuge from American racism while a graduate student, as symptomatic of the racism entrenched in Western civilization.

During the doctor's initial time in Atlanta the remainder of the family stayed in New York. His daughter, Yolanda, who had briefly married Harlem's famous poet, Countee Cullen, had remarried Arnett Williams and given birth to a baby girl, Du Bois Williams, a couple of years before Du Bois left the NAACP. Nina, Yolanda, and the baby stayed in the Harlem apartment after he moved back down South. The baby and Nina joined Du Bois in Atlanta for a brief period, from 1938 to 1939, after Yolanda moved to Baltimore with her husband. The marriage, however, dissolved fairly quickly after the move, and Nina and Du Bois Williams relocated to a four-bedroom home near the Morgan State College campus in Baltimore.

While Du Bois was in Atlanta, the world once again went to war. During World War II, he did not take the same approach he had during the first world conflict. He stood staunchly against the war, proclaiming to Andrew J. Allison of Fisk University that he refused "to believe that there is any excuse for the United States to enter the present war." Du Bois, like many African

Americans, agreed with author, journalist, and satirist George S. Schuyler when he said, "Our war is not against Hitler in Europe, but against the Hitlers in America." On that pacific front, Du Bois thought race prejudice was central to American hostility toward Japan and stated that the "British Empire has caused more human misery than Hitler will cause if he lives a hundred years." After the bombing of Pearl Harbor and America's entry into the war, Du Bois altered his position and argued that black America had to support the effort. The support was not passively provided, however. In 1942 he opined in the *Amsterdam News*, "We sadly admit today that the First World War did not bring us democracy. Nor will the second. . . . We close ranks again but only, now as then, to fight for democracy and democracy not only for white folk but for yellow, brown and black."

A truer democracy was the one outcome Du Bois desired from the conflict, but he was not optimistic for such a change. As he wrote in 1940, "The democracy which the white world seeks to defend does not exist." He did not think worldwide democracy could be achieved unless it was "applied to the majority of people." "Democracy is tapping the great possibilities of mankind from unused and unsuspected reservoirs of human greatness," he argued. If oppressed people were "released from poverty, ignorance and disease," world peace would be possible. "There will be no need to fight for food, for healthy homes, for free speech," Du Bois reasoned, "for these will not depend on force, but increasingly on knowledge, reason and art."

This "Du Boisian intellectual idealism," as biographer David Levering Lewis calls it, drove the scholar-activist into yet another stage of his life and career. The Board of Trustees of Atlanta University recommended that Du Bois, at the age of seventy-six, "be retired from the active faculty." The retirement age of the university was sixty-five, but he had returned to academia at that threshold and before the school had adopted a mandatory retirement provision. Needless to say, Du Bois was surprised by the actions of the board, "without a word of warning." He explained in his *Autobiography*, "I found myself at the age of 76 without employment and with less than $5,000 of savings." The situation was particularly critical because of his recent purchase of the home in Baltimore. Du Bois appealed to the university alumni and the black community more broadly for support and in short order was offered positions at Howard University, North Carolina College for Negroes, and his alma mater, Fisk. Additionally, after protests, Atlanta's trustees agreed to give Du Bois a year's salary and a pension.

In the midst of this crisis Du Bois was unexpectedly asked to return to the NAACP. The association's board had voted to ask him to accept a "full or part time" position to prepare "material to present on behalf of the American Negro and colored peoples of the world to the Peace Conference." After some negotiations Du Bois accepted the offer to become director of special research, with the intent to collect data "concerning peoples of Africa and their descendants."

He thought this was an opportunity to get back into the organization and do some good work, but some in the organization believed it was more of a ceremonial position for the elder scholar-activist. As Du Bois explained, the NAACP leadership believed he would be content to be a ghostwriter for Walter White, to "act as window dressing, say a proper word now and then, and give the Association and its Secretary moral support." The seventy-six-year-old doctor, of course, had different plans, and thus began another set of turbulent years between Du Bois, White, and the NAACP.

Du Bois's initial work with the organization was tied to the association's involvement in creating the United Nations. As the war was concluding, he had begun to push for the United States to support anticolonial actions. Du Bois was disappointed that he could not get the Roosevelt and Truman administrations to take such a position but initially believed that the newly forming UN would support independence movements in Africa, the Caribbean, and Asia. Du Bois was sadly mistaken. After attending the founding conference in San Francisco as a representative of the NAACP, he was quick to condemn the proceedings, which he charged had effectively precluded the representation of 750 million peoples in the organization.

Du Bois's frustration was carried over into his anti-imperialist book, *Color and Democracy: Colonies and Peace* (1945), which was published a short time after the initial meeting of the UN. In his analysis Du Bois was skeptical that the new international body would succeed as an instrument of peace, because

insofar as such efforts leave practically untouched the present imperial ownership of disfranchised colonies, and in this and other ways proceed as if the majority of men can be regarded mainly as sources of profit for Europe and North America, in just so far we are planning not peace but war, not democracy but the continued oligarchical control of civilization by the white race.

In October, Du Bois traveled to Manchester, England, for the sixth Pan-African Congress. This meeting had been called by George Padmore and followed a meeting in Harlem that Du Bois had organized in collaboration with Paul Robeson, Max Yergan, and Alphaeus Hunton of the Council on African Affairs. Both meetings pressed the anti-imperialist message that Du Bois, and at this stage, the NAACP had been promoting. The Manchester meeting was extremely interesting because of who attended, a literal past and future of the pre- and postwar nationalist movements that would lead the anti-imperialist independence movements of the later twentieth century: Amy Jacques-Garvey and Norman Manley of Jamaica, Jomo Kenyatta of Kenya, Wallace Johnson of Sierra Leone, and Mangus Williams of Nigeria. Kwame Nkrumah, who also attended the Harlem meeting, represented Ghana, and, of course, Padmore represented Trinidad. Du Bois was honored by the delegation as the father of Pan-Africanism. The two hundred delegates drafted resolutions calling for political action. They condemned poverty, illiteracy, and starvation of African peoples, all of which they saw as endemic to colonialism. They demanded the right to organize labor unions and called for home rule. As Du Bois explained, "It is perfectly clear . . . what the African peoples want. They want the right to govern themselves. . . . We must impress upon the world that it must be Self Government."

Once he returned to the United States, Du Bois began working on a written appeal to the UN's Commission on Human Rights. The petition, *An Appeal to the World: A Statement on the Denial of Human Rights to Minorities in the Case of Citizens of Negro Descent in the United States of America and an Appeal to the United Nations for Redress*, was a collection of essays drafted by Du Bois, Earl Dickerson, Milton Konvitz, William R. Ming, Leslie S. Perry, and Rayford W. Logan. It gained the endorsement of Padmore and many of the international delegates from the Pan-African Congress, as well as Mary McLeod Bethune, Adam Clayton Powell Jr., and D. W. Jemison of the National Baptist Convention. Du Bois wanted to work with Robeson, Yergan, and the Council on African Affairs, but he explained that the NAACP, or White in particular, was fearful of their connection to the Communist Party. When the resolution was brought before the UN's Human Rights Commission, the Soviet Union supported hearings on its subject matter. The United States did not, and the petition died on the floor. Former first lady Eleanor Roosevelt, the U.S. delegate on the Human Rights Commission and a member of the NAACP board, explained to Du Bois that the petition on American racism "would be embarrassing; that it would be seized upon by the Soviet Government." The Cold War was heating up, and geopolitics trumped racial justice.

Throughout the same year Du Bois continued to push his anti-imperialist positions, focusing particularly on the continent of Africa. From March 1947 to March 1948 he published fifty-one essays on African politics for the New York–based *People's Voice* newspaper. In 1947 he also produced a new book, *The World and Africa: An Inquiry into the Part Which Africa Has Played in World History*, a reproach of Western capitalist rule over nonwhite people. "If the nation could not exist half slave and half free," Du Bois declared, "then the world in which this nation plays a larger and larger part also cannot be half slave and half free, but must recognize world democracy. . . . The iron curtain was not invented by Russia; it hung between Europe and Africa half a thousand years." The book was incredibly influential in anticolonialist circles; as Robeson explained, "*The World and Africa* was one of the first important books on modern postwar Africa and helped to point out and focus attention on the continuing exploitation of Africa by the 'free world.'"

In the mid-to-late 1940s Du Bois kept up a rigorous speaking schedule, especially for a man in his seventies. In 1946 he spoke in Montgomery, Alabama; Knoxville, Tennessee; Philadelphia; Columbia, South Carolina; New York City; and before the Southern Negro Youth Congress, lecturing on the necessity of Soviet and American cooperation and the relationship between democracy and the perpetuation of racism. In New York, for instance, he insisted that "no attack upon social problems by free democratic methods" could occur in the United States as long as a color line existed. America's democratic ideals, argued Du Bois, were compromised by the government's "alliance with colonial imperialism and class dictatorship in order to enforce the denial of freedom to the colored peoples of the world."

The following year, before the NAACP convention in Washington, D.C., Du Bois pressed upon the delegates the importance of addressing the issues of world poverty and colonial rule. "Socialism is an attack on poverty. We can by our knowledge, by the use of our democratic power, prevent the concentration of political and economic power in the hands of the monopolists who rule colonies," he asserted. "Every leading land on earth is moving toward some form of socialism, so as to restrict the power of wealth, introduce democratic methods in industry, and stop the persistence of poverty and its children, ignorance, disease and crime." The June address was Du Bois's last major speech before an NAACP convention. Even though Du Bois was not a Communist, in the shifting geopolitical world any left position was often construed as a Soviet-inspired scheme.

A few months before Du Bois's address, historian Arthur Schlesinger Jr. warned in *Life* magazine that the Communists were "sinking tentacles" into the NAACP. Michigan governor Kim Sigler also red-baited the organization, proclaiming that the group was nothing more than a "communist front." Initially, Walter White stood strong against the accusations, but in early 1947 and early 1948 some individuals associated with the NAACP were fired or denied federal posts because of their perceived political affiliations. Additionally, in 1947 the southern conference of the association passed a resolution that voiced their opposition to "communism or communist tactics."

As the Cold War between the United States and the Soviet Union intensified and anticommunist sentiment in the country continued to rise, Walter White thought it sensible to soften the anti-imperialist rhetoric of the association. Moreover, with Truman's support of civil rights, as seen with the organization of his commission and his support of their recommendations, *Secure These Rights*, and his administration's move toward desegregation of the armed forces, White saw it practical for the organization to align itself more closely to Truman and the Democratic Party. All of this action put Du Bois in a difficult position and in particular placed his June speech to the NAACP convention even more outside the developing positions of the association.

Tensions between White and Du Bois continued to rise during the election of 1948. Despite their lukewarm cooperation around the UN over the preceding few years, the two NAACP leaders still did not like each other. Du Bois complained that White did not provide enough office space upon his return—his office, housing three workers, was twelve feet by twenty feet and contained two desks, a typing table, six file cabinets, and 2,500 books, among other items. He also believed that White "wanted me visibly at his elbow so that at no point could my subordination to him be doubted." Moreover, he took exception to the secretary's policy of having all incoming mail opened by the office staff, even personal correspondence, before being delivered to the recipient. Du Bois seethed that the NAACP, the organization he had helped to create, had become "a rigid dictatorship, virtually under the control of one man."

During the election of 1948 Walter White wanted the organization to support Harry S. Truman and the Democratic Party, but Du Bois was surprised to find out that a majority of the national office "favored Wallace," the Progressive Party candidate. He was quick to remind the national staff of the long-standing nonpartisan position of the organization, which prohibited members from speaking at meetings or promoting "partisan activity." Du

Bois, however, maintained open support for Wallace, and White continued to complain about his actions, which "bewildered" and frustrated the older activist. As Du Bois explained to friend Arthur Spingarn when he was invited to return to the NAACP, "There was no warning that my usual freedom of expression was to be curtailed, except of course general conformity with the NAACP program." All in all it continued to strengthen Du Bois's notion that the association was no longer a democratic organization.

A few months before the election, another skirmish between White and Du Bois would lead to the second and final parting of the ways for Du Bois and the NAACP. White asked Du Bois to draft a memorandum for the Paris UN meeting. The doctor refused "to comply" and offered a lengthy written response to the secretary and the remaining board members. In his letter, he complained that the NAACP had not taken a position against the "reactionary, war-mongering colonial imperialism of the present administration." He further warned that it would be a mistake for the association "to be loaded on the Truman bandwagon, with no chance for opinion or consultation. . . ." In essence Du Bois was not pleased with the shift the organization was taking, the increasing anticommunist, non-anti-imperialist position White had moved the group forward in an effort to align it with the Truman administration and the Democratic Party. Du Bois's letter was leaked to the *New York Times* a few days after he sent the memo to the board. The paper did not print all of Du Bois's criticisms, but it aired enough of his grievances. After the contents became public, the NAACP board quickly met and voted to terminate Du Bois's employment by the end of the year.

Du Bois had become a casualty of the Cold War. Cold War ideology demanded that African Americans limit their political and civil affiliations with the American nation and the ideas of democracy and capitalism. While a majority of the NAACP's leadership was willing to duck for cover in this environment, Du Bois was not willing to limit his expressions or actions. After his address and his refusal to play by the orders of White, the leaders of the association had decided that Du Bois and his views did not align with their shifting positions. Technically they said it was insubordination when he refused "to cooperate" with White when asked for a memorandum. Additionally, they accused Du Bois of going public, though he denied it, with the criticisms of the NAACP before the board fully considered the document.

Once again Du Bois found himself outside the organization he helped create. Moreover, the eighty-year-old was without a job and was in financial straits. In 1945 Nina was injured in a fall and had to undergo surgery and physical therapy. The following year she suffered a stroke that paralyzed her left side. At the time of his dismissal the medical costs were $2,600 a year. He had his small retirement pension from Atlanta University, but it would not cover expenses plus housing, food, clothing, travel, and so on. After his dismissal the NAACP had also agreed to pay the elder activist a pension, but it too, once combined with his meager royalties and Atlanta University stipend, would not cover all his expenses.

Many activists, educators, editors, and general supporters of the association openly and privately deplored the removal of Du Bois and sought to assist him in gaining financial assistance and possibly a new position. One of the main individuals in this activity was Shirley Graham, daughter of civil rights activist and AME minister D. A. Graham, who was an activist, artist, playwright, and writer in her own right. She had gained notoriety for her plays in the 1930s, including an opera named *Tom-Tom*, and her popular biographies of Frederick Douglass and George Washington Carver, to name a few. In 1947 she gained more of a name for herself when she was awarded a prestigious fellowship from the Guggenheim Foundation. "It seemed as if she was marching from triumph to triumph," explained biographer Gerald Horne.

After Du Bois's removal Graham organized the Emergency Committee for Dr. Du Bois and the NAACP with support from numerous African American leaders, including Alain Locke, E. Franklin Frazier, and Horace Mann Bond. They encouraged Du Bois to lead a national campaign to reorganize the NAACP. He wanted nothing to do with it but did accept Paul Robeson's invitation to serve as honorary vice chairman of the Council of African Affairs.

With the moving of his books and files from the cramped NAACP office to a space at the council's Manhattan headquarters, Du Bois once again set out on a different path. Since the creation of the NAACP, he and the organization had worked tirelessly to fight discrimination and injustice in America. Though it had been a tough fight, the organization and its allies were making an impact. For a number of people, however, Du Bois was no longer a figure that embodied that struggle. Many within the community looked upon him as a person who should step aside and relax his efforts, letting younger activists, many whom had grown up on his words and actions, to take the lead. As he later noted, "I would have been hailed with approval if I had died at 50. At 75 my death was practically requested." Dr. Du Bois, however, was not built to step aside. The world was moving, and so was one of its greatest intellectuals. In 1948, Eastern Europe and China had joined the Communist political experiment. Moreover, after the end of the war and the U.S. bombing of Hiroshima and Nagasaki, the prospect of global nuclear war became more frighteningly real. Additionally, the colonial world was rebelling against its European rulers, and the possibility of a politically independent Africa was becoming more than a fantasy. The United States was clearly standing against these tectonic shifts in the geopolitical world. W. E. B. Du Bois believed that if the nation accepted this stance without critical analysis and consultation, we were headed toward "a tragic mistake." At the age of eighty the sage scholar-activist was not going to sit around passively and allow the world to transform without a passing word. His position in the Council of African Affairs, and the connections with its supporters, provided Du Bois with a new platform from which he could speak truth to power. This new stage marked a phase of his life in which he never ceased to battle for peace.

Chapter Six

Marching toward Peace

As, then, a citizen of the world as well as of the United States of America, I claim the right to know and tell the truth as I see it. I believe in Socialism as well as Democracy. I believe in Communism . . . I despise men and nations which judge human beings by their color, religious beliefs or income. I believe in free enterprise among free men and individual initiative under physical, biological and social law. I hate War.

—W. E. B. Du Bois, 1952

Being fired from the organization he had helped create was certainly difficult for the elder scholar-activist, but the removal from the NAACP also freed him to participate in the national and international peace movements against the growing Cold War as well as the independence movements developing in the colonial world. This activity would occupy the remainder of his life. The aging Du Bois would continue a strenuous publishing regimen. During the period he would also work with numerous groups, suffer loss, be dragged into the spotlight during the nation's obsession with purging the United States of all Communists and their allies, and finally leave the country to reside in an independent nation on the continent of Africa.

Joining Robeson, Alphaeus Hunton, Ralph Bunche, journalist Charlotta Bass, and others in the Council of African Affairs, a group founded in 1937 that disseminated information about Africa in the United States, energized the scholar. The council could not pay Du Bois, but he used the small group of activists and the council itself as the launching pad for the struggles of his final years: anticolonialism, anti-imperialism, and the spread of socialism. During his time with the organization he wrote numerous articles for their publication, *New Africa*, and penned a column, "As the Crow Flies," for the *Chicago Globe* along with dozens of other pieces for a number of journals, including the *National Guardian*.

When Du Bois joined the council, it was in a bit of disarray. J. Howard McGrath, the U.S. attorney general, had just placed the group on its list of "subversive" organizations, which led to the resignation of one of its founders, Max Yergan, and litigation by Yergan against other leaders of the council. Despite this activity, which seriously hampered the organization's work, Du Bois explained that he joined the group because he believed in the work the council "should do" for Africa. Additionally, he explained in 1951 that "no man or organization" should be denied a voice "because of political or religious beliefs."

Around the same time he joined forces with the council, Du Bois was asked to participate in the Cultural and Scientific Conference for World Peace. Sponsored by over five hundred prominent scholars and artists, the conference met in New York from March 25 to 27, 1949. Among those in attendance were Alexander A. Fadeyev, secretary of the Soviet Writer's Union; Louis Untermeyer; Norman Mailer; Marlon Brando; Arthur Miller; Leonard Bernstein; Pablo Neruda; Frank Lloyd Wright; F. O. Matthiessen; Shirley Graham; and Howard Fast. In his remarks concluding the mass rally at Madison Square Garden, Du Bois told the attendees that "the dark world is on the move," and they did not want revenge but rather peace and a world free of racism. Du Bois himself wanted not only a world free of racism, but also freedom of thought for all global citizens. He believed that allowing individuals the freedom to think, to live free of intellectual "barbarism," would help the world become a better place. He believed that it was an important moment in history, that "this instant" humanity stood "tiptoe on the threshold of infinite freedoms, freedoms which outstretch this day of slavery as the universal sun out-measures our little earthly system. . . . Even the chained and barred fields of work and food and disease today will yield vaster freedoms when men are let to think and talk and explore more widely in regions already really free."

Intellectual "barbarism" continued, however, as Cold War antagonism grew and the arms race between the United States and the USSR proliferated. Both sides of the Cold War were ramping up their rhetoric and stifling open discussion about divergent views of the world. This situation filled Du Bois with a certain amount of urgency, which would lead him to travel in 1949 to two separate peace conferences, one in Paris and one in Moscow.

Figure 6.1. W. E. B. Du Bois and Paul Robeson shaking hands at the World Peace Conference in Paris. Courtesy University of Massachusetts Archives.

In April, Du Bois led the American delegation, including among others Paul Robeson and Shirley Graham, to the World Congress of the Defenders of Peace. Robeson grabbed the headlines when he proclaimed, "The black folk of America will never fight against the Soviet Union." In his address, Du Bois, who received a tremendous welcome from the delegates when he was announced, told the attendees that socialism was spreading throughout the world and that colonialism was the real enemy of America, which was leading and defending the practice. "Drunk with power," he stated, "we are leading the world to hell . . . and to a Third World War."

Robeson and Du Bois returned to Cold War–frenzied America as political outcasts. In reaction to his comments a number of groups canceled previously scheduled concerts and public lectures. Walter White attacked Robeson and his speech in *Negro Digest*. Du Bois published a rebuttal, but it had little effect on the mood and sentiment of the nation. Du Bois himself also suffered from his statements in Paris. Before his trip he had been invited to give the commencement address at Morgan State College. Shortly after his return college president Martin D. Jenkins wrote Du Bois to cancel. "Your appearance with Mr. Paul Robeson," Jenkins explained, "and, particularly, your failure to condemn his treasonable statement made at that meeting have linked you in the public mind with the Communist movement in this country."

A few months after his return from Europe and his being marked with the scarlet letter, Du Bois appeared before the House Committee of Foreign Affairs to testify against the Truman administration's request to finance the North Atlantic Treaty Organization and its moves to suppress leftist movements in Turkey and Greece. In his remarks Du Bois warned Congress that a blank check would not allow the United States to "decide when and where to fight." A few weeks later Du Bois traveled to the Soviet Union, his third trip to the Communist-led nation, for the All-Soviet Peace Conference. Finding a more receptive audience than in the halls of the U.S. government earlier in the month, Du Bois, the only American representative, declared, "I represent millions of citizens of the United States who are just as opposed to war as you are." In his comments he revisited arguments made in *Black Reconstruction* about race, labor, and the creation of America. He suggested that America's peace movement was directly related to its ability to redefine democracy. "No great American industry admits that it could or should be controlled by those who do not work. But unless democratic methods enter industry, democracy fails in other paths of life." According to Du Bois, the only way to achieve peace and equality for blacks in America was "for the American people to take control of the nation in industry as well as government."

A few months after his return Du Bois became the chairman of the Peace Information Center (PIC), a new organization whose purpose was "to tell the people of the United States what other nations were doing and thinking about war." Among other things, the center began circulating the "Stockholm Appeal," a petition to abolish atomic weapons. The petition would eventually gain more than two million signatures, a number that could not be ignored by the federal government and a number that brought increased scrutiny to the center, its members, and their activities.

While he and the PIC began their work and the United States went to war on the Korean peninsula, Du Bois lost his beloved wife of forty-four years. Nina Du Bois died on July 1, 1950, after five difficult years of pain and suffering following a stroke. In an action that had to be incredibly hard and painful, Du Bois trekked up to Great Barrington, Massachusetts, to bury Nina next to their son, Burghardt, who had died nearly a half-century before. After the experience, the eighty-two-year-old reflected on loss and loneliness; he had now buried a son, a wife, and so many colleagues. "I was lonesome because so many boyhood friends had died, and because a certain illogical reticence on my part had never brought me many intimate friends," he observed. New friends came to his aid. George Padmore sent his condolences, as did many others, including Shirley Graham, who was becoming his closest friend, confidant, and coworker.

Du Bois, however, did not have much time to grieve. With the PIC gaining support for its antinuclear activities, the government looked to discredit the group. On July 12, less than two weeks after Nina's death, Secretary of State Dean Acheson launched the first volley. The secretary called the Stockholm petition "a propaganda trick in the spurious 'peace offensive' of the Soviet Union." Du Bois replied in a press statement, "Must any proposals for averting atomic catastrophe be sanctified by Soviet opposition? . . . Today in this country it has become standard reaction to call anything 'communist' and therefore subversive and unpatriotic, which anybody for any reason dislikes. We feel strongly that this tactic has already gone too far; that it is not sufficient today to trace a proposal to a communist source in order to dismiss it with contempt." In response to Du Bois's statement and the success of the Stockholm Appeal the federal government infiltrated and investigated the PIC.

Du Bois quickly found out the implications of such actions. He was scheduled to attend the Bureau of World Partisans of Peace meeting in Prague and began to make the necessary arrangements to travel abroad. The State Department slowed down the process and ultimately restricted Du Bois's passport "to 60 days in Czechoslovakia and 'necessary lands' en route, and 'not to be validated for additional countries without the express authorization of the Department of State.'" Du Bois stated that he "felt like a prisoner on parole," but in reality America was increasing its Cold War paranoia, and his actions were falling under what was now being deemed subversive.

Du Bois was well aware of the geopolitical chess game he was now a part of and, accordingly, addressed the subject in his Prague speech.

> For 50 years I have been in touch with social currents in the United States. Never before has organized reaction wielded the power it does today: by ownership of press and radio, by curtailment of free speech, by imprisonment of liberal thinkers and writers. It has become almost impossible today in my country even to hold a public rally for peace. This has been accomplished by

inducing Americans to believe that America is in imminent danger of aggres-
sion from communism, socialism and liberalism, and that the peace movement
cloaks this threat.

Manifestly, to meet this hysteria, it is not so much a question of the
concept of war under any circumstances, as the far deeper problem of getting
the truth to the masses of the citizens of the United States who still in over-
whelming majority hate murder, crippling destruction and insanity as a means
of progress. By personal contact, by honest appeal, by knowing the truth
ourselves, we can yet win the peace in America. But it is going to take guts and
willingness to jeopardize jobs and respectability.

Before leaving Czechoslovakia Du Bois received two very different tele-
grams. First the American Labor Party sent a cablegram asking him to run as
its candidate for the U.S. Senate. The second message was informational.
The PIC sent word informing their chairman that the Justice Department had
requested that the center register as "agents of a foreign principal." The first
cable he found comical, the second he believed was nothing more than intimidation. In response to the act of intimidation, Du Bois stated the government
did not "indicate on whose behalf we are supposed to be acting." The PIC,
according to Du Bois, was "an entirely American organization devoted to the
cause of world peace."

After initially laughing off the first telegram, Du Bois, "knowing well
from the first" that he had no chance to win and that the campaign would
bring him "ridicule at best and jail at worst," nonetheless agreed to run for
the Senate. Du Bois considered the campaign to be about two things. First, by
operating as an outside candidate he seemed to think that he somehow would
aid Vito Marcantonio, a radical congressman from New York, in his bid for
the Senate seat; second, and more simplistically, the campaign was a mode to
get his opinion out to the public. As Du Bois commented in 1952 in his *In
Battle for Peace*, "I found myself increasingly proscribed in pulpit, school
platform. My opportunity to write for publication was becoming narrower
and narrower, even in the Negro press. I wondered if a series of plain talks in
a political campaign would not be my last and only chance to tell the truth as
I saw it."

With little press, and seemingly no real budget, Du Bois set out on the
campaign trail. In the fall of 1950 he canvassed the state, giving ten major
addresses and a number of radio broadcasts. The campaign held mass events
throughout New York City's boroughs, with stops in Harlem, the Bronx,
Brooklyn, and Queens. In October, seven thousand people gathered for a

Figure 6.2.   Group portrait of Du Bois and other American Labor Party candidates taken in 1950 when Du Bois ran for the U.S. Senate. Courtesy University of Massachusetts Archives.

rally at Madison Square Garden. At the event Du Bois pushed his campaign themes of peace and civil rights. "The most sinister evil of this day," he told the audience, "is the widespread conviction that war is inevitable and that there is no time left of discussion. . . . In modern world war all contestants lose and not only lose the immediate causes of strife, but cripple the fundamental bases of human culture."

Du Bois did not win, nor did Marcantonio for that matter, but the aging scholar-activist found it gratifying that he received over two hundred thousand votes, gaining his highest success in the black communities of New York. As with many of his life experiences, success did not always matter. It was the analysis during or after the moment that had lasting lessons, and his venture into electoral politics was no different. In early 1951, a few months after the election, Du Bois evaluated his experience in an address at Yale University's law school. As he explained to his audience, in the world's leading democracy, members of Congress are not elected by majority vote. South Carolina and Connecticut had the same number of congressmen, he outlined, but in South Carolina they needed "100,000 votes" to elect theirs, while "it took 800,000" to win in Connecticut. His own electoral total, he observed, was far greater than many southern "Dixiecrats" (those southern Democrats who seceded from their party in 1948) who held powerful positions in Congress. In the end Du Bois believed that America "never has been a democracy. . . . Our industrial enterprise is dominated by vast monopolies and our freedom of thought increasingly chained by law, police spies and refusal to let anybody earn a decent living who does not think as he is told to think."

These words may have resonated even more a month later. Throughout the fall and during his senatorial run, the State Department continually demanded that the PIC register "as an agent of foreign principal." Du Bois continued to resist, and after the group disbanded in October he believed the action was no longer necessary because the PIC no longer existed. The government did not see it the same way. They repeatedly requested registration and finally organized a grand jury to investigate possible indictments against PIC members. On February 9, 1951, less than twenty days before Du Bois's eighty-third birthday, the group was indicted for failure to register, naming five defendants: Elizabeth Moos, Sylvia Soloff, Abbott Simon, Kyrle Elkin, and Du Bois. All faced the possibility of a $10,000 fine and five years in a federal penitentiary.

In Cold War America, the fear of Communism was driving the country to criticize all departures from traditional thinking and condemn all new questioning in any field of thought. According to Gerald Horne, Du Bois's "ideas on peace and civil rights were not new, but given the frigid political climate they were adventurous and questing." In the end the indictment was as much real as a terror tactic to intimidate black America. If the government would prosecute the elderly Du Bois, there was no doubt they would go after anyone who dared to speak out for peace, civil rights, or anything else for that matter.

Upon the news of the indictment, Du Bois and Shirley Graham hurried their wedding plans. Shirley Graham had been one of Du Bois's closest companions since he returned to the NAACP in 1944. She assisted him in finding an apartment when he returned to New York. Graham was also one of the main individuals who introduced and exposed Du Bois to the larger left and progressive activist circles. As David Graham Du Bois explained years later, his mother "gradually drew Dr. Du Bois into contact with leading figures of [the] new progressive movement. . . . In his presence, they behaved like disciples at the feet of the prophet. Slowly Dr. Du Bois found these white Americans to be of a different breed from those who early in his career had discouraged him from seeking out or desiring white company." Two days before his arraignment the two were married. As Graham later recalled, "This, I knew was no time for maiden coyness. . . . With him in jail, only a wife could carry the case to the people. *I must be in a position to stand at his side*—this I felt was essential."

The arraignment of the indicted peace activists, including the newlywed Du Bois, occurred on February 16 in the Federal District Court in Washington, D.C. As Du Bois recalled, "The proceedings were brusque and unsympathetic. We were not treated as innocent people whose guilt was to be inquired into, but distinctly as criminals whose innocence was to be proven, which was assumed to be doubtful." During the arraignment he collectively but defiantly read a statement: "It is a sad commentary that we must enter a courtroom today to plead Not Guilty to something that cannot be a crime—advocating peace and friendship between American people and the peoples of the world. . . . In a world which has barely emerged from the horrors of the Second World War and which trembles on the brink of an atomic catastrophe, can it be criminal to hope and work for peace?"

Following the arraignment, where bail was set for $1,000, the group was sent for processing. As Du Bois later remembered,

> Following the arraignment I was told to follow the marshal, and walk down some narrow stairs at the back of the courtroom into a small basement room, perhaps ten feet square. There I was fingerprinted and asked details as to my life and work; told to remove my coat and empty my pockets, and then examined carefully by an orderly for concealed weapons! As I turned around to go upstairs where the matter of bail was to be arranged, the marshal put handcuffs on me and Mr. Elkins, so that for ten minutes we were manacled together. Then a stir and murmur rose sharply from behind the grated partition where the public could look through and see what was happening. I heard one of our attorneys protesting sharply. The marshal grumbled, looked disconcerted, but finally unlocked our handcuffs, and we walked out into the corridor.

After the ordeal in the basement of the courthouse, bail was quickly posted and Du Bois and the other defendants were released. The whole incident, however, had shaken the elderly scholar-activist. As he remembered, "I have faced during my life many unpleasant experiences; the growl of a mob; the personal threat of murder; the scowling distaste of an audience. But nothing so cowed me as that day . . . when I took my seat in a Washington courtroom as an indicted criminal."

Out on bail, Du Bois quickly discovered the real politics of being indicted in Cold War America. The Council of African Affairs had planned a celebration for his eighty-third birthday to be held at the Essex House in New York City. E. Franklin Frazier agreed to be the chairman, and a number of individuals agreed to be honorary chairs, including Mary Church Terrell, Mary White Ovington, Mordecai Johnson, Alain Locke, and Rabbi Abba Hillel Silver of the Zionist Organization of America. The whole atmosphere and sentiment leading up to the event was celebratory, so many wanted to gather to mark the birth of the dogged activist. After the indictment of the PIC officers the mood quickly changed. The press had tried and convicted the activists, and in the pages of the nation's dailys without a court ruling and individuals quickly moved to disassociate themselves with Du Bois and the event. Three of the scheduled speakers, Rabbi Silver, Mordecai Johnson, and Charlotte Hawkins Brown, president of Palmer Memorial Institute, all withdrew. Both Nobel Peace Prize recipient Ralph Bunche, and Du Bois's old NAACP ally, Arthur Spingarn, suddenly found themselves unable to attend. Finally the Essex House canceled the contract. The tenacious Du Bois became weary. "I can stand a good deal," he later stated, "but this experience was rather more than I felt like bearing, especially as the blows continue to fall."

Graham, Robeson, and Frazier pressed on, securing a smaller place, Small's Paradise in Harlem, and successfully held a celebration on February 23. The festive event included seven hundred attendees and numerous domestic and foreign well-wishers, standing defiantly by Du Bois and affirming their commitment to world peace and social justice. Du Bois thanked Frazier for standing beside him and emphasized: "We are still in of course for the rather nasty fight in the matter of this indictment, but are going to fight to the end. It's a big opportunity and I am willing to go to jail in order to make the courts face the issue and make the United States and especially Negro Americans know what they are up against."

After the celebration Du Bois and his friends began preparing for the trial. They also started organizing support committees. The black community was slow to get on board. As Du Bois explained, "At first many Negroes were puzzled. They did not understand the indictment and assumed that I had let myself be drawn into some treasonable acts or movements in retaliation for continued discrimination in this land, which I had long fought." The behavior of the NAACP's leadership was nasty in its comments and lack of support for their former colleague. Arthur Spingarn, whom Shirley Graham Du Bois called on directly for support, stated that "of course the Soviet Union was furnishing funds for the Peace Information Center," although he thought there was a possibility that Du Bois was unaware of the money. Despite the opinions of the NAACP leadership, branches of the organization called for the group to support Du Bois. Walter White, however, ignored the branch pressure and continually assured the board and membership that he had "irrefutable proof" that Moscow supported the PIC, evidence that he repeatedly claimed came directly from the attorney general's office. In light of this claim and general board sentiment, the national office ordered the locals "not to touch" the case or send support to Du Bois. Not all of them listened, however, and ultimately their pressure forced the board of directors to pass a weak, noncommittal resolution.

> Without passing on the merits of the recent indictment of Dr. Du Bois, the board of directors of the NAACP expresses the opinion that this action against one of the great champions of civil rights lends color to the charge that efforts are being made to silence spokesmen for full equality of Negroes. The board also reaffirms its determination to continue its aggressive fight for full citizenship rights for all Americans.

Despite the confusion and general reluctance of many, some individuals did come to the aid and support of Du Bois. Fisk University's Charles S. Johnson became the only black university president to express his support. One of the most powerful statements of support came from Langston Hughes. In his *Chicago Defender* column he wrote,

> Somebody in Washington wants to put Dr. Du Bois in jail. Somebody in France wanted to put Voltaire in jail. Somebody in Spain sent Lorca, their greatest poet, to death before a firing squad. Somebody in Germany under Hitler burned the books, drove Thomas Mann into exile, and led their leading Jewish scholars to the gas chamber. Somebody in Greece long ago gave Socrates the hemlock to drink. Somebody at Golgotha erected a cross and somebody drove the nails into the hands of Christ. Somebody spat on his garments. No one remembers their names."

After numerous delays, on November 8, 1951, Du Bois and his codefendants again appeared in federal court. The government's case was extremely weak, actually in many ways a sham. The case rested on the claim that the center had "acted as an agent or in a capacity similar to that for a foreign organization or foreign political power." There was no way the government could prove this, so what they were left to do was to try to prove subversion by association. As Judge Matthew F. McGuire explained to the prosecution:

> I am not trying any propaganda lines. I am not trying any foreign policy questions involving any country, including our own. You have a very simple case here. You charged this Peace Information Center and these individuals, as officers and directors, as being agent of a foreign principal, and disseminating propaganda in the United States. You have got to show a tie-up between the principal so-called and the so-called agent. If you don't do that, you are out of court.

Ultimately, the Justice Department could not prove any connection, and immediately after the government rested, Vito Marcantonio, the defense counsel and of course Du Bois's opponent for the Senate run, who had volunteered his legal services, moved for dismissal of all charges. To the surprise of many, with Marcantonio not calling one witness, Judge McGuire agreed with the defense and a verdict of acquittal for the defendants. David Levering Lewis has argued that the trial was a political miscalculation by the government, with the elderly Du Bois appearing as a sympathetic figure as a defendant. Some believed that the Truman administration influenced the judge's decision after determining that a conviction would reflect badly on it, as would have Albert Einstein's testimony; he had agreed to appear as a character witness for Du Bois.

Du Bois stepped out of the trial a free man, but the government had succeeded in doing its damage to his reputation. The nation's most well-known civil rights activist had been called a Communist sympathizer and for the majority of the nation, white or black, the accusation, in the era of the McCarran and Smith Acts, was enough to convict no matter what a judge decided in a courtroom. As Gordon B. Hancock, of Virginia Union University, argued, "It was a shame that Dr. Du Bois, the Negro champion, almost had to bear his cross alone. . . . Negroes who claim to be race champions and crusaders and fighters and leaders and uncompromisers to the last ditch actually deserted Dr. Du Bois in the hour of his greatest trial."

For the remainder of his life Du Bois continued to suffer the consequences of the trial. Within Cold War America he became increasingly isolated from the black community, as many of the leadership took anticommunist positions and Du Bois's work become more and more imbued with Marxist thought. During the year of the trial the NAACP reduced his pension by half, from $2,400 to $1,200. He and Shirley were denied visas to Brazil when they tried to attend a peace conference, because their "proposed travel would be contrary to the best interests of the United States." Shortly thereafter, Canada denied entry to the two activists as they attempted to travel to the Canadian Peace Congress, where Du Bois was scheduled to speak.

Publishers also began to turn away from one of the most prolific American writers of the twentieth century. Harcourt, Brace and Company, publishers of five of his books, *Darkwater, Dark Princess, Black Reconstruction, Dusk of Dawn*, and *Color and Democracy*, rejected a new manuscript, "America and Russia." Additionally, a number of periodicals which previously had published his work, including *New Republic, Journal of Negro Education, Foreign Affairs*, and the *American Journal of Sociology*, no longer requested pieces from the now-marked scholar.

The whole situation was in many ways surreal. Du Bois was not a member of the Communist Party and had not committed any crime. Yet he was "rejected of men, refused the right to travel abroad and classed a 'controversial figure' even after being acquitted of guilt by a Federal court of law." Over a decade later, in his posthumously published book, *The Autobiography*, one can see how much the experience wounded Du Bois and how that wound continued to fester until his death. "It was a bitter experience," he recalled,

> and I bowed before the storm. But I did not break. I continued to speak and write when and where I could. I faced my lowered income and lived within it. I found new friends and a wider world than ever before—a world with no color line. I lost my leadership of my race. It was a dilemma for the mass of Negroes; either they joined the current beliefs and actions of most whites or they could not make a living or hope for preferment. Preferment was possible. The color line was beginning to break. Negroes were getting recognition as never before. Was not the sacrifice of one man, small payment for this? Even those who disagreed with this judgment at least kept quiet. The colored children ceased to hear my name.

For the first few years after the trial Du Bois and Shirley Graham, with the State Department deciding that it "would be contrary to the best interests of the United States" for either of them to have a passport, led a quiet life in their Brooklyn home. Du Bois pushed for amnesty for all who were convicted under the Smith Act. He continued to write a vigorous amount, particularly on the topics of peace, third-party politics, and African liberation, even though his publishing outlets narrowed greatly because of his "reputed Communist front affiliations." In 1953 the State Department requested a sworn statement from Du Bois and Shirley Graham as to whether they were "now or ever had been communists." Both refused, with Du Bois infuriatedly replying in the press that his political beliefs "are none of your business."

As time progressed, Du Bois watched with excitement and great interest as the civil rights movement began to unfold after the May 17, 1954, Supreme Court ruling in the *Brown v. Board of Education* decision, which outlawed the idea of "separate but equal" in education. He saw the decision as a great step forward toward "complete freedom and equality between black and white Americans," but he believed black Americans had to "go further" to achieve full justice. As he stated, "The Supreme Court decision on segregation in schools called for a distinct modification of my attitude toward segregation which I expressed in 1934." He assumed that legal discrimination would have lasted much longer and praised NAACP leadership and its legal team for fighting so "valiantly and intelligently in the courts" when he had "little faith in substantial victory." Du Bois warned, however, that the "battle was not won." He reminded his readers that the United States had a "long habit of ignoring and breaking the law. Especially in the South, lawlessness is common and has been for a century." Du Bois predicted that the movement for change would continue but questioned what would happen during the "25 or 50 years while the southern South [*sic*] refuses to obey the law." What will happen to Negro children? He still urged the black community to take hold of the education of the children. Du Bois believed, as he had argued in the 1920s and 1930s, that even with "successfully mixed schools," African American children would be forced to "suffer for years from southern white teachers, from white hoodlums who sit beside them and under school authorities . . . who hate and despise them." Despite these difficulties, Du Bois believed that full desegregation had to be supported, as part of "the price of liberty."

Du Bois also started reviewing the civil rights leadership that began to develop in the wake of *Brown v. Board.* He praised Martin Luther King Jr. but also noted limitations to his nonviolent methods. "Among normal human beings," he argued, "non-violence is the answer to the temptation to force. . . . no normal human being of trained intelligence is going to fight the man who will not fight back. In such cases," he explained, "peace begins and grows just because it is. But suppose they are wild beasts or wild men," he prodded his readers. "We have today in the South millions of persons who are pathological cases," he argued. "They are not normal and cannot be treated as normal." Given this reality, Du Bois doubted that white southerners were adept enough to respond to nonviolent tactics. "So long as people insult, murder and hate, by hereditary teaching, non-violence can bring no peace. It will bring migration until that fails, and then attempts at bloody revenge. It will spread war and murder." This is why he questioned the NAACP and Martin Luther King Jr.'s repudiation of Robert Williams, the NAACP leader from North Carolina, who was alleged to have used weapons and engaged in a kidnapping, when he called for the use of self-defense if necessary. He was sorry, Du Bois explained, to see King and other leaders oppose "the young colored man in North Carolina who declared that in order to stop lynching and mob violence, Negroes must fight back."

As a consequence of the rise of the civil rights movement, many activists and scholars began to look back at the long struggle and in the process rediscovered Du Bois's central role and voice. Along with this recognition, Du Bois's reputation as a race leader gradually began to be restored. A number of local associations and black universities began to invite him for lectures. This was a huge shift for an individual who only a couple of years before was denied the right to speak at an American Labor Party rally because of his affiliations with Communist organizations. In 1958 his undergraduate alma mater, Fisk University, named a campus dormitory after him and bestowed him with an honorary degree. In the same year he traveled to Washington, D.C., to lecture at Howard University. Two years later, Morgan State, the school that had dropped his lecture in the midst of accusations of his Communist affiliations, awarded him an honorary degree and again invited him to speak at commencement.

The NAACP did not share in the renewed interest in the civil rights pioneer, however. Though Walter White was gone, passing in 1955, his successor, Roy Wilkins, still thoroughly anticommunist and anti-left, continued to isolate the organization's founder and intellectual mentor. Du Bois was not asked to contribute to a special issue of *The Crisis* in 1957 on the Gold Coast. When asked about the omission by a member of the association, Wilkins explained, "There is no policy to exclude Dr. Du Bois . . . however I would be less than frank if I did not say that the present views of Dr. Du Bois are not deemed fitting" for the NAACP journal. Wilkins's statements occurred at the same time Du Bois struggled, to no avail, to get his passport returned so he could attend the independence ceremonies of the Gold Coast after a personal invitation from Kwame Nkrumah. The State Department, Vice President Richard Nixon, and black congressmen Charles Diggs, William Dawson, and Adam Clayton Powell Jr. all failed to assist in getting Du Bois's passport reinstated.

Upon hearing the news that "one of the fathers of the Pan-African movement" was not going to be able to attend the ceremony, the editors of the Ghana *Evening News* expressed their shock and anger. "To deny" Du Bois, a Pan-African father, "the right to see the birth of the child of his dreams . . . is to precipitate the end of the venerable scholar—a veritable fratricide. . . . Du Bois has been in chains before. Again he is in psychological chains. We wish him the fortitude to bear, at his ripe age of 89, the newly forged shackles of man's inhumanity to man."

The following year, the judicial branch forced the government to remove the shackles. In 1958 the Supreme Court ruled that Congress had never given the State Department any authority to demand a political affadavit as prerequisite to issuing a passport. Paul Robeson, after an eight-year battle, regained his passport and quickly left for Europe. The Du Boises received their passports in July and promptly planned a trip abroad with a hastened departure after learning that the Eisenhower administration was pressing Congress to pass legislation to nullify the court's ruling. Upon leaving the shores of the United States on August 8, 1958, Du Bois noted that he "felt like a released prisoner."

Dr. Du Bois and Shirley Graham traveled the world for nearly a year, spending time in France, England, Sweden, Germany, Czechoslovakia, the Soviet Union, and China. While in Czechoslovakia, he received an honorary degree from Charles University in Prague. He was pleasantly surprised by the honor, because he believed the majority of the white institutions of higher learning in America did not know who he was or did not value his scholarship. In his acceptance address, "The American Negro and Communism," Du Bois noted, "The salvation of American Negroes lies in socialism." He believed that a growing number of African Americans would support the expansion of the "welfare state" and "favor strict regulation of corporations or their public ownership." The following month, while in Communist East Berlin reliving his schoolboy days, he received another honorary degree, this time from Humboldt University, formerly Berlin's Kaiser Friedrich Wilhelm University.

The couple later traveled to the Soviet Union, where they would stay for five months. While there, he received the International Lenin Prize for his "indefatigable activities in promoting relations of stable friendship and cooperation among all peoples of the world." He also sat down with Prime Minister Nikita Khrushchev for a two-hour discussion about "peace and ways to develop closer friendlier relations with the United States," he told the readers of the *National Guardian*. "I talked about Africa," he explained. "Africans are just beginning to think of themselves as Africans and it must be encouraged. I thought the best way the Soviet Union could help would be to study African history, African culture, African environment, and make the results of their studies available to the African people." According to Du Bois, he suggested that the best way to do this was to develop an institute that would "aim at the promotion of scientific research" on the "cultural, political, and economic organizations" of the peoples of Africa. By the end of the year Khrushchev established an "Institute on Africa" within the Soviet Union's national Academy of Sciences.

During his journeys Du Bois also violated the State Department's travel ban by passing into the People's Republic of China, his second trip; he had traveled there in 1936. While in China, he celebrated his ninety-first birthday on the radio in Peking, and he and Shirley Graham spent three months traveling throughout the country. Du Bois held meetings with, among others, Mao Tse-tung and Prime Minister Chou Enlai. After their meeting Mao declared to the nation, "Du Bois [is] a great man of our time. His deeds of heroic struggle for the liberation of the Negroes, his outstanding achievements in academic fields and his sincere friendship toward the Chinese people will forever remain in the memory of the Chinese people." According to Du Bois, he had "never seen a nation which so amazed and touched me as China." A few months after returning to the United States, the couple's passports were again seized by the State Department and would be held until mid-1960.

Trapped back in the United States, Du Bois continued to write, drafting his *Autobiography* and the last volume of his *The Black Flame* trilogy, a collection of three novels: *The Ordeal of Mansart* (1957), *Mansart Builds a School* (1959), and *Worlds of Color* (1961), which he first began drafting in 1948. He also traveled the country, giving a number of public lectures. One of the most significant was given at the University of Wisconsin in May 1960. There Du Bois began to address how the past year, as he explained to E. Franklin Frazier, "was a most extraordinary journey" and had changed his "outlook on current affairs." He told the audience that he used to believe that democracy and socialism were both equal forms of government if they were practiced fairly. After his travels, however, he had concluded that socialism was "the most successful form of government" possible today. Capitalism, according to Du Bois, had become "a force so destructive, that it cannot be endured." Du Bois encouraged the leaders of the civil rights movement to understand the current state of affairs. Their tactics, according to the seasoned activist, did not "reach the center of the problem." He wanted them to look beyond the desegregation struggle. African Americans must "insist upon the legal rights which are already theirs, and add to that, increasingly a socialistic form of government, an insistence upon the welfare state." The movement also had to check the power of "corporations which monopolize wealth." As Du Bois told an audience at Johnson C. Smith College in North Carolina the month before, African Americans needed to lead the fight for socialism in America, and in doing so, "restore the democracy of which we [the United States] have boasted so long and done so little."

Shortly after these addresses Du Bois and Shirley Graham were able to obtain their passports to travel to Ghana to attend Nkrumah's presidential inauguration ceremony as his personal guests. While in Accra, where they stayed for six weeks, Nkrumah asked Du Bois to revive his idea of creating an *Encyclopedia Africana*, with the project headquartered in Ghana. Initially, the ninety-two-year-old scholar balked at the idea, but after some consideration, and before he left the country for Nigeria to attend the inauguration of Nnamdi Azikiwe, Du Bois accepted the offer.

Upon returning to the states, he began nearly full-time work on the *Encyclopedia*. He began contacting a number of scholars with expertise in African, Caribbean, and African American Studies. In April 1961 Du Bois outlined a tentative schedule for the project, with the first volume projected to appear "not later than 1970," when he would be 102 years old. He thought he would continue to work on the project from Brooklyn and move to Accra sometime the following year. Du Bois's plans, however, were sped up.

After the federal court ruling declared that the Communist Party would have to register under the Subversive Control Act, Du Bois and Shirley Graham feared their passports would again be seized by the State Department. The Du Boises then urgently asked Nkrumah if they could come to Ghana earlier than planned and began to plan their departure. Du Bois entrusted most of his private papers and unpublished material with historian and confidant Herbert Aptheker. Then in October 1961 Du Bois made one last political act. For more than a decade Du Bois had suffered from America's increasingly anticommunist repression, but he had never joined the Party, and according to Aptheker, "Du Bois had come to the decision that the program and ideas of the Communist Party of the United States were nearest to his own ideas." According to Aptheker, "with the warlike policy of Washington and its policy of persecuting radicals and Communists," Du Bois "decided that it might be some contribution to peace and sanity if he were not only to join the Party but to do with a public announcement of the fact." So on October 1, 1961, Du Bois applied for membership to the Communist Party.

In his letter of application to Gus Hall, the Party's leader in the United States, Du Bois stated, "I was early convinced that Socialism was an excellent way of life, but I thought it might be reached by various methods. For Russia," he explained, "I was convinced she had chosen the only way open to her at the time. I saw Scandinavia choosing a different method, half-way between Socialism and Capitalism. In the United States I saw Consumers Cooperation as a path from Capitalism to Socialism, while England, France and Germany developed in the same direction in their own way. After the depression and the Second World War, I was disillusioned. The Progressive movement in the United States failed. The Cold War started. Capitalism called Communism a crime." Du Bois therefore had come to the "firm conclusion" that "Capitalism cannot reform itself; it is doomed to self-destruction. No universal selfishness can bring social good to all. Communism . . . is the only way of human life. . . . I want to help bring that day." Four days later he and Shirley Graham departed for Accra.

Upon their arrival and after settling into their "beautiful seven-room residence," Du Bois set to work on the *Encyclopedia* project. He selected as his assistant Alphaeus Hunton Jr., the son of his Council of African Affairs colleague, who was at the time teaching in Guinea. In May 1962 Du Bois was officially named the secretariat of the project, and things seemingly were moving forward as planned, but for the elderly scholar his age and failing health were increasingly getting in his way.

In 1962 Du Bois underwent a series of surgeries, one a painful prostate operation in London. After the procedure he demonstrated incredible resiliency for a ninety-four-year-old as he convalesced in Switzerland and later in China for several months. Du Bois resumed work in late 1962 and planned a trip back to the United States but was denied a passport renewal because of his affiliation with the Communist Party. As a member of the Party, he could not legally possess a passport and could be imprisoned up to ten years for his

Figure 6.3. Du Bois at home on the evening of his ninety-fifth birthday toasting President Kwame Nkrumah and his wife, Fathia Rizk Nkrumah. Courtesy University of Massachusetts Archives.

perceived crime. Given the circumstances, therefore, Du Bois was a man without a country, until February 17, six days before his ninety-fifth birthday. He renounced his American citizenship and became a citizen of Ghana, upon which he stated:

> My great-grandfather was carried away in chains from the Gulf of Guinea. I have returned that my dust shall mingle with the dust of the forefathers. There is not much time left for me. But now my life will flow on in the vigorous, young stream of Ghanaian life which lifts the African personality to its proper place among men. And I shall not have lived and worked in vain.

New citizenship, however, could not stop time. In March 1963 Du Bois reluctantly retired from the *Encyclopedia* project as he accepted that he could no longer perform his duties as the secretariat. Over the next several months his health continued to deteriorate, and finally death came on August 27, 1963. The following day acknowledgment of his death came across the Atlantic Ocean to Washington, D.C., where a quarter of a million Americans gathered for the March on Washington for Jobs and Freedom. Roy Wilkins, the executive secretary of the NAACP, made the announcement, honoring his predecessor at *The Crisis* for his fearless activism, even though Wilkins held the memory of the civil rights stalwart at arm's length for his leftward movement in his final years.

The following day in Ghana, Nkrumah and the nation mourned the death of the Pan-Africanist with a state funeral. "We mourn the death of Dr. William Edward Burghardt Du Bois, a great son of Africa," declared Nkrumah in his radio-broadcasted eulogy. "He was an undaunted fighter for the emancipation of colonial and oppressed people, and pursued this objective throughout his life. . . . It was the late George Padmore," he continued, "who described Dr. Du Bois as the greatest scholar the Negro race has produced, and one who always upheld the right of Africans to govern themselves."

Representatives from around the world sent their respects, including every embassy and consulate in Accra, except for the United States. The U.S. government, like Roy Wilkins, allowed geopolitics to dictate its response. P. L. Prattis, however, properly placed the situation into context in his September 7, 1963, eulogy for the *Pittsburgh Courier*:

> There will be those who will deplore the fact that he became a Communist and left his native land. I do not. . . . Many men have left their native lands for reasons less onerous than those Dr. Du Bois may have had. The Puritans, after Cromwell, left their native land for Holland and sneaked out of Holland to come to the American colonies. Except for the Negroes, the United States is made up of people who left their native lands all over the globe. So far as Dr. Du Bois' joining the Communist Party is concerned, he could not fail to remember that when he was 83 years old he had been handcuffed, fingerprinted and tried for an alleged political offense. He was not found guilty. What does such do to the pride of a proud man? . . . . I laud him because he fought and worked until the last moment before he was taken away.

Many in America certainly concurred with Prattis's assessment. The doctor, the voice of the race for nearly a century, had passed. Author John Oliver Killens commented on the sorrow he, Sidney Poitier, and James Baldwin mutually expressed when they heard the news at the march. "The old man died . . . and not one of us asked what old man? We all knew [who the old man was] because he was our old man. He belonged to every one of us. And we belonged to him. To some of us he was our patron saint, our teacher and our major prophet."

Five years later, Martin Luther King Jr. pointedly stated at the Carnegie Hall tribute to Du Bois, held on the centennial of Du Bois's birth: "Dr. Du Bois has left us, but he has not died. The spirit of freedom is not buried in the grave of the valiant." The titan had passed, but like John Brown, the man Du Bois wrote about in 1909, his "soul goes marching on." He dedicated his life to justice, freedom, the obliteration of the idea of racial inferiority, and most of all, to Africans throughout the Diaspora. Generations throughout the globe, but particularly in the United States, had been raised on his words, thoughts, and ideas. As he had hoped, his ideas long surpassed his life in memory and significance in the struggle for justice and equality in American life.

W. E. B. Du Bois was a remarkable man, an intensely original and independent thinker, and a writer who elegantly demanded that America and the world recognize the humanity of African-descended people throughout the globe. He was a scholar who pressed for humanity to stand up for global racial justice and an activist who called for America and governments throughout the world to create real democracy that defended the rights of all of its citizens. The best way to honor the man and his legacy is to examine the totality of his thought and actions, to not limit one's examination and analysis to one part of his life or one phrase of his written or spoken words. Amid all the tragedy in the world, Du Bois believed in progress and had hope for the future. As he stated in his "Last Message to the World," the eulogy he penned in 1957, "Believe in life! Always human beings will live and progress to greater, broader and fuller life." Du Bois's greatest legacy was his belief that we human beings could create a better world, a just world, and a world of genuine democracy.

A Note on Sources

Several archival collections proved useful in preparing this study of the life and thought of W. E. B. Du Bois, particularly the W. E. B. Du Bois collection at the University of Massachusetts-Amherst. Additional collections consulted included the National Association for the Advancement of Colored People Papers and the Booker T. Washington Papers at the Library of Congress.

The body of scholarship related to W. E. B. Du Bois is daunting and is increasing all the time. What follows is a list of many of the general works that have been particularly illuminating in the preparation of this biography. Because of the enormous collection of work on Du Bois, topical sources are outlined for each chapter. The best full-length biography of W. E. B. Du Bois is the stunning two-volume work by David Levering Lewis, *W. E. B. Du Bois: Biography of a Race, 1868-1919* (New York: H. Holt, 1993) and *W. E. B. Du Bois: The Fight for Equality and the American Century, 1919-1963* (New York: H. Holt, 2000), which was crucial in writing this book. In addition to the indispensable Lewis biographies, countless others are necessary reading to understand Du Bois's life and intellectual thought, the best of which include Elliot Rudwick's *W. E. B. Du Bois: A Study in Minority Group Leadership* (Philadelphia: University of Pennsylvania Press, 1960); Manning Marable's *W. E. B. Du Bois, Black Radical Democrat* (Boston: Twayne, 1986); Gerald Horne's *Black and Red: W. E. B. Du Bois and the Afro-American Response to the Cold War, 1944-1963* (Albany: State University of New York Press, 1986); Arnold Rampersad's *The Art and Imagination of W. E. B. Du Bois* (New York: Schocken Books, 1990); and Raymond Wolters's

Du Bois and His Rivals (Columbia: University of Missouri Press, 2002). There are also a number of interesting thematic biographical studies of Du Bois, including Edward J. Blum's *W. E. B. Du Bois, American Prophet* (Philadelphia: University of Pennsylvania Press, 2007); Derrick P. Alridge's *The Educational Thought of W. E. B. Du Bois: An Intellectual History* (New York: Teachers College Press, 2007); Keith Byerman's *Seizing the Worlds; History, Art, and the Self in the Work of W. E. B. Du Bois* (Athens: University of Georgia Press, 1994); Shamoon Zamir's *Dark Voices: W. E. B. Du Bois and American Thought, 1888-1903* (Chicago: University of Chicago Press, 1995); Adolph L. Reed's *W. E. B. Du Bois and American Political Thought: Fabianism and the Color Line* (New York: Oxford University Press, 1997); Gerald Horne's *W. E. B. Du Bois: A Biography* (Santa Barbara, CA: Greenwood Press, 2010); and Amy Bass's *Those About Him Remained Silent : The Battle over W. E. B. Du Bois* (Minneapolis: University of Minnesota Press, 2009).

Readers may explore a number of edited volumes of Du Bois's speeches and newspaper and magazine articles, as well as some of his private correspondence, in a number of anthologies and edited volumes that have been published since the 1970s. *The Seventh Son: The Thought and Writings of W. E. B. Du Bois*, ed. Julius Lester (New York: Random House, 1971); *W. E. B. Du Bois Speaks: Speeches and Addresses, 1890-1919*, ed. Philip S. Foner (New York, London: Pathfinder Press, 1970); *W. E. B. Du Bois Speaks: Speeches and Addresses, 1920-1963*, ed. Philip S. Foner (New York, London: Pathfinder Press, 1970); *W. E. B. Du Bois*, ed. William M. Tuttle Jr. (Englewood Cliffs, NJ: Prentice-Hall, 1973); *A W. E. B. Du Bois Reader*, ed. Andrew G. Paschal (New York: Collier Books, 1993); *The Oxford W. E. B. Du Bois Reader*, ed. Eric J. Sundquist (New York: Oxford University Press, 1996); *W. E. B. Du Bois: A Reader*, ed. David L. Lewis (New York: H. Holt, 1995); W. E. B. Du Bois, *Against Racism: Unpublished Essays, Papers, Addresses, 1887-1961*, ed. Herbert Aptheker (Amherst: University of Massachusetts Press, 1985); *The Correspondence of W. E. B. Du Bois, Vol. 1: 1877-1934,* ed. Herbert Aptheker (Amherst: University of Massachusetts Press, 1973); *The Correspondence of W. E. B. Du Bois, Vol. 2: 1934-1944,* ed. Herbert Aptheker (Amherst: University of Massachusetts Press, 1976); and *The Correspondence of W. E. B. Du Bois, Vol. 3: 1944-1963,* ed. Herbert Aptheker (Amherst: University of Massachusetts Press, 1978). Readers may also access the growing online collection of Du Bois's papers at the University of Massachusetts-Amherst digital collection Credo. The web address is http://credo.library.umass.edu/view/collection/mums312.

W. E. B. Du Bois's two fully developed autobiographies, *Dusk of Dawn: An Essay Toward an Autobiography of a Race Concept* (New York: Harcourt, Brace and Co., 1940) and *The Autobiography of W. E. B. Du Bois: A Soliloquy on Viewing My Life from the Last Decade of Its First Century* (New York: International Publishers, 1968), are excellent sources of information on his life and career. In addition, readers should consult the various newspapers and journals Du Bois edited or contributed to throughout his long career. Most important among these is *The Crisis* magazine, the official organ of the National Association for the Advancement of Colored People, which he edited from 1910 to 1935. An overview of these published works is found in the anthologies listed above as well as the wonderful edited collections of Herbert Aptheker: *Writings by W. E. B. Du Bois in Non-Periodical Literature Edited by Others* (Millwood, NY: Kraus-Thomson, 1982); *Writings by W. E. B. Du Bois in Periodicals Edited by Others, Vol. 1: 1891-1909* (Millwood, NY: Kraus-Thomson, 1982); *Writings by W. E. B. Du Bois in Periodicals Edited by Others, Vol. 2: 1910-1934* (Millwood, NY: Kraus-Thomson, 1982); *Writings by W. E. B. Du Bois in Periodicals Edited by Others, Vol. 3: 1935-1944* (Millwood, NY: Kraus-Thomson, 1982); and *Writings by W. E. B. Du Bois in Periodicals Edited by Others, Vol. 4: 1945-1961* (Millwood, NY: Kraus-Thomson, 1982). A final indispensable volume is Aptheker's comprehensive bibliography of Du Bois's writings, *Annotated Bibliography of the Published Writings of W. E. B. Du Bois* (Millwood, NY: Kraus-Thomson, 1973).

Finally, no study of Du Bois is complete without the numerous non-autobiographical monographs he published throughout his lifetime. These include *The Philadelphia Negro* (Philadelphia: University of Pennsylvania, 1899); *The Souls of Black Folk* (Chicago: A. C. McClurg and Company, 1903); *John Brown: A Biography*, ed. John David Smith (1909; rpt., Armonk, NY: M. E. Sharpe, 1997); *The Negro* (New York: H. Holt, 1915); *Darkwater: Voices from within the Veil* (New York: Harcourt, Brace and Howe, 1920); *The Gift of Black Folk* (Boston: Stratford, 1924); *Africa, Its Geography, People and Products* (New York: Haldeman-Julius, 1930); *Black Reconstruction: An Essay toward a History of the Part Which Black Folk Played in the Attempt to Reconstruct Democracy in America, 1860-1880* (New York: Russell & Russell, 1935); *Black Folk Then and Now: An Essay in the History and Sociology of the Negro Race* (1939; rpt., New York:

Octagon Books, 1970); *Color and Democracy: Colonies and Peace* (New York: Harcourt Brace, 1945); *The World and Africa: An Inquiry into the Part Which Africa Has Played in World History* (New York: The Viking Press, 1947); *In Battle for Peace: The Story of My 83rd Birthday* (New York: Masses & Mainstream, 1952); and *An ABC of Color* (New York: International Publishers, 1969). In addition, see Du Bois's literary works, *The Quest of the Silver Fleece: A Novel* (Chicago: A. C. McClurg & Co., 1911); *Dark Princess: A Romance* (New York: Harcourt Brace, 1928); *The Ordeal of Mansart, Vol. 1 of The Black Flame Trilogy* (New York: Mainstream, 1957); *Mansart Builds a School, Vol. 2 of The Black Flame Trilogy* (New York: Mainstream, 1959); and *Worlds of Color, Vol. 3 of The Black Flame Trilogy* (New York: Mainstream, 1961).

PREFACE

The following sources were referred to for the preface: W. E. B. Du Bois, "Fifty Years After," preface to the Jubilee Edition of *The Souls of Black Folk* (New York: Blue Heron Press, 1953); W. E. B. Du Bois, *W. E. B. Du Bois: A Reader*, ed. Meyer Weinberg (New York: Harper & Row, 1970); and W. E. B. Du Bois, *The Oxford W. E. B. Du Bois Reader*, ed. Eric J. Sundquist (New York: Oxford University Press, 1996).

CHAPTER 1

This chapter utilized Du Bois's *The Autobiography of W. E. B. Du Bois*, his 1940 *Dusk of Dawn*, and the collection of essays *The Souls of Black Folk*. In addition, information for this section drew from the Du Bois Papers; Aptheker's collection of Du Bois's early newspaper columns, *Newspaper Columns, Vol. 2: 1883-1944* (White Plains, NY: Kraus-Thomson, 1986); and unpublished material, *Against Racism: Unpublished Essays, Papers, Addresses, 1887-1961*, ed. Herbert Aptheker (Amherst: University of Massachusetts Press, 1985), as well as Du Bois's essay, "My Evolving Program for Negro Freedom," in *What the Negro Wants*, ed. Rayford Logan (Chapel Hill: University of North Carolina Press, 1944). In addition, the chapter drew from a number of biographies on Du Bois, including Lewis's *W. E. B. Du Bois: Biography of a Race*; Marable's *W. E. B. Du Bois, Black Radical Democrat*; Rudwick's *W. E. B. Du Bois: A Study in Minority Group Leadership*; and Rampersad's *The Art and Imagination of W. E. B. Du Bois*. Also referred to is John Henrik Clarke, Esther Jackson, Ernest Kaiser, and J. H. O'Dell, eds., *Black Titan: W. E. B. Du Bois: An Anthology* (Boston: Beacon Press, 1970). An article by Kenneth D. Barkin, "'Berlin Days,' 1892-1894: W. E. B. Du Bois and German Political Economy," *Boundary 2* 27, no. 3 (2000): 79–101, and one by Axel R. Schafer, "W. E. B. Du Bois, German Social Thought, and the Racial Divide in American Progressivism, 1892-1909," *Journal of American History* 88, no. 3 (2001): 925–49, provided some additional context for Du Bois's time in Germany. Other books that provided context on the black experience in the post-emancipation era are Leon F. Litwack's *Been in the Storm So Long: The Aftermath of Slavery* (New York: Knopf, 1979) and *Trouble in Mind: Black Southerners in the Age of Jim Crow* (New York: Alfred A. Knopf, 1998); Rayford Whittingham Logan's *The Betrayal of the Negro: From Rutherford B. Hayes to Woodrow Wilson* (1965; rpt., New York: Da Capo Press, 1997); Joel Williamson's *The Crucible of Race: Black/White Relations in the American South since Emancipation* (New York: Oxford University Press, 1984); August Meier's *Negro Thought in America, 1880-1915: Racial Ideologies in the Age of Booker T. Washington* (Ann Arbor: University of Michigan Press, 1963); and Shawn Leigh Alexander's *An Army of Lions: The Civil Rights Struggle before the NAACP* (Philadelphia: University of Pennsylvania Press, 2012).

CHAPTER 2

In addition to the biographies by Lewis, Marable, Rudwick, and Rampersad, this chapter drew upon Derrick P. Alridge's *The Educational Thought of W. E. B. Du Bois: An Intellectual History* (New York: Teachers College Press, 2007); Du Bois's autobiographies *Dusk of Dawn* and *The Autobiography*; *The Philadelphia Negro: A Social Study*, ed. Elijah Anderson (Philadelphia: University of Pennsylvania Press, 1996); *The Suppression of the African Slave-Trade to the United States of America, 1638-1870* (1896; rpt., New York: Russell & Russell, 1965); and the collection of essays *The Souls of Black Folk*. A number of Du Bois's individual pieces were also important in understanding his actions and intellectual thought during this period. These included select essays in Aptheker's edited volume *Against Racism*, as well as "The Training of Negroes for Social Power," *Outlook* 75 (1903): 409–14; "Of the Training of Men," *Atlantic Monthly* 90 (1902): 289–97; "The Talented Tenth," in *The Negro Problem; A Series of Articles by Representative American Negroes of To-day* (New York: J. Pott & Co., 1903), 33–75; "The

Negroes of Farmville, Virginia: A Social Study," *Bulletin of the United States Department of Labor* III (1898): 1–38; *The Conservation of Races* (American Negro Academy Occasional Papers, No. 2, 1897); "Strivings of the Negro People," *Atlantic Monthly* 80, no. 478 (1897): 194–98; "A Negro Schoolmaster in the New South," *Atlantic Monthly* 83 (1899): 99–104; and "Litany of Atlanta," *Independent* 61 (1906): 856–58. Additionally, a few collections of Du Bois's writings proved useful not only for the works included but also the overall framing of his thought by the editors. These included *W. E. B. Du Bois on Sociology and the Black Community*, ed. Dan S. Green and Edwin D. Driver (Chicago: University of Chicago Press, 1978); Robert Wortham, *W. E. B. Du Bois and the Sociological Imagination: A Reader, 1897-1914* (Waco, TX.: Baylor University Press, 2009); W. E. B. Du Bois and Robert Wortham, *The Sociological Souls of Black Folk: Essays* (Lanham, MD: Lexington Books, 2011); and W. E. B. Du Bois and Eugene F. Provenzo, *Du Bois on Education* (Lanham, MD: Rowman & Littlefield, 2002).

Several books and essays provided background information and context. These included Michael B. Katz and Thomas J. Sugrue's edited *W. E. B. Du Bois, Race, and the City: The Philadelphia Negro and Its Legacy* (Philadelphia: University of Pennsylvania Press, 1998); Elliott M. Rudwick's "W. E. B. Du Bois and the Atlanta University Studies on the Negro," *Journal of Negro Education* 26, no. 4 (1957): 466–76; Earl Wright's "W. E. B. Du Bois and the Atlanta University Studies on the Negro, Revisited," *Journal of African American Studies* 9, no. 4 (2006): 3–17; and Clarence A. Bacote's *The Story of Atlanta University: A Century of Service, 1865-1965* (Atlanta: Atlanta University, 1969).

Alfred A. Moss's *The American Negro Academy: Voice of the Talented Tenth* (Baton Rouge: Louisiana State University Press, 1981) is still the definitive book on the American Negro Academy. For an understanding of the fuller context of the Atlanta Riot, readers can see Gregory Mixon's *The Atlanta Riot: Race, Class, and Violence in a New South City* (Gainesville: University Press of Florida, 2005) and David Fort Godshalk's *Veiled Visions: The 1906 Atlanta Race Riot and the Reshaping of American Race Relations* (Chapel Hill: University of North Carolina Press, 2005). For Du Bois's specific reaction, Dominic J. Capeci Jr. and Jack C. Knight's essay, "Reckoning with Violence: W. E. B. Du Bois and the 1906 Atlanta Race Riot," *Journal of Southern History* 62, no. 4 (1996), is a nice overview.

CHAPTER 3

In addition to the biographies by Lewis, Marable, Rudwick, and Rampersad, this chapter drew upon Du Bois's autobiographies *Dusk of Dawn* and *The Autobiography* as well as the collection of essays *Souls of Black Folk*. In addition, it drew from his essays "The Negro Problem from a Negro Point of View: V. The Parting of the Ways," *The World To-day* 6, no. 4 (1904): 521–23; "To Solve the Negro Problem," *Collier's* 33 (1904): 14; "Hopeful Signs for the Negro," *Advance* 44 (1902): 327–28; "Possibilities of the Negro," *Booklover's Magazine* 2, no. 1 (1903): 3–15; "Debit or Credit," *The Voice of the Negro* 2, no. 1 (1905): 677; and "Litany of Atlanta," *Independent* 61 (1906): 856–58.

Numerous pages have been published on *The Souls of Black Folk*. For this chapter I consulted Ernest Allen Jr.'s essay "Du Boisian Double Consciousness: The Unsustainable Argument," *Massachusetts Historical Review* 43 (2002): 217–53; Robert Gooding-Williams's *In the Shadow of Du Bois: Afro-Modern Political Thought in America* (Cambridge, MA: Harvard University Press, 2009); Stephanie J. Shaw's *W. E. B. Du Bois and the Souls of Black Folk* (Chapel Hill: University of North Carolina Press, 2013); Bernard W. Bell, Emily Grosholz, and James B. Stewart's edited *W. E. B. Du Bois on Race and Culture: Philosophy, Politics, and Poetics* (New York: Routledge, 1996); Keith Byerman's *Seizing the World: History, Art, and the Self in the Work of W. E. B. Du Bois* (Athens: University of Georgia Press, 1994); and Robert B. Stepto's *From Behind the Veil: A Study of Afro-American Narrative* (Urbana: University of Illinois Press, 1979).

For more on Du Bois's relationship with Booker T. Washington, August Meier's *Negro Thought in America* is still essential, as well as Louis R. Harlan's two-volume biography, *Booker T. Washington: The Making of a Black Leader, 1856-1901* (New York: Oxford University Press, 1972) and Harlan's *Booker T. Washington: The Wizard of Tuskegee, 1901-1915* (New York: Oxford University Press, 1983). See also Raymond Smock's biography, *Booker T. Washington: Black Leadership in the Age of Jim Crow* (Chicago: Ivan R. Dee, 2009), and Wolter's *Du Bois and His Rivals*. Harlan's multivolume collection of Washington's papers, Louis R. Harlan and Raymond Smock, eds., *The Booker T. Washington Papers* (Urbana: University of Illinois Press, 1972), and the Library of Congress collection of his papers were also consulted for this chapter. In addition, Robert Norrell's newer *Up from History: The Life of Booker T. Washington* (Cambridge: Harvard University Press, 2009) places the debate into a larger context of the times, and James D. Anderson's *The Education of Blacks in the South, 1860-1935* (Chapel Hill: University of North Carolina Press, 1988) provides the context for the southern educational system from the Civil War to the 1930s.

Additional context on the period and individuals is available in Alexander's *An Army of Lions*; Ray Stannard Baker's *Following the Color Line: American Negro Citizenship in the Progressive Era* (New York: Harper Torchbooks, 1964); Stephen R. Fox's *The Guardian of Boston: William Monroe Trotter* (New York: Atheneum, 1970); Patricia Sullivan's *Lift Every Voice: The NAACP and the Making of the Civil Rights Movement* (New York: New Press, 2009); Paula Giddings's *Ida: A Sword among Lions* (New York: Amistad, 2008); and Mia Bay's *To Tell the Truth Freely: The Life of Ida B. Wells* (New York: Hill and Wang, 2010).

CHAPTER 4

In addition to the biographies by Lewis, Marable, Rudwick, Wolters, and Rampersad, and Du Bois's autobiographies *Dusk of Dawn* and *The Autobiography*, this chapter consulted his writings in *The Crisis* magazine; *Darkwater: Voices from within the Veil* (New York: Harcourt, Brace and Howe, 1920); "Reconstruction and Its Benefits," *American Historical Review* 15 (1910): 781–99; "The African Roots of War," *Atlantic Monthly* 115 (1915): 707–14; *The Quest of the Silver Fleece: A Novel* (Chicago: A. C. McClurg & Co., 1911); *The Negro* (New York: H. Holt, 1915); *Dark Princess: A Romance* (New York: Harcourt, Brace and Company, 1928); and *The Gift of Black Folk* (Boston: Stratford, 1924).

A number of works were used to help frame the historical context around the Harlem Renaissance, including Ernest Allen Jr.'s essential "The New Negro: Explorations in Identity and Social Consciousness, 1910-1922," in *1915: The Cultural Moment: The New Politics, the New Woman, the New Psychology, the New Art, and the New Theater in America*, ed. Adele Heller and Rudnick Lois (New Brunswick, NJ: Rutgers University Press, 1991), 48–68; David Levering Lewis's *When Harlem Was in Vogue* (New York: Oxford University Press, 1979); and Lewis's edited volume *The Portable Harlem Renaissance Reader* (New York: Penguin Books, 1994), which contains Du Bois's essay "Criteria for Negro Art" and his critique of Carl Van Vechten's *Nigger Heaven*. Also of great use was George Hutchinson's *The Harlem Renaissance in Black and White* (Cambridge: Harvard University

Press, 1995); Mark R. Schneider's *African Americans in the Jazz Age: A Decade of Struggle and Promise* (Lanham, MD: Rowman & Littlefield, 2006); and Alain Locke's collection *The New Negro* (New York: Atheneum, 1992).

Several books provided information on Marcus Garvey and the UNIA, beginning with Marcus Garvey's *Philosophy and Opinions of Marcus Garvey*, ed. Amy Jacques-Garvey (1923-1925; rpt. New York: Atheneum, 1969) and Robert A. Hill's edited *The Marcus Garvey and Universal Negro Improvement Association Papers* (Berkeley: University of California Press, 1983). Three Garvey biographies were also useful: Edmund David Cronon's *Black Moses: The Story of Marcus Garvey and the Universal Negro Improvement Association* (Madison: University of Wisconsin Press, 1955); Tony Martin's *Race First: The Ideological and Organizational Struggles of Marcus Garvey and the Universal Negro Improvement Association* (Westport, CT: Greenwood Press, 1976); and Colin Grant's *Negro with a Hat: The Rise and Fall of Marcus Garvey* (New York: Oxford University Press, 2008). Also helpful were Mary G. Rolinson's *Grassroots Garveyism: The Universal Negro Improvement Association in the Rural South, 1920-1927* (Chapel Hill: University of North Carolina Press, 2007) and Wilson Jeremiah Moses's *Creative Conflict in African American Thought: Frederick Douglass, Alexander Crummell, Booker T. Washington, W. E. B. Du Bois, and Marcus Garvey* (New York: Cambridge University Press, 2004).

For context on Pan-Africanism and Du Bois's relationship to the movement, chapters in Bernard W. Bell, Emily Grosholz, and James B. Stewart's edited *W. E. B. Du Bois on Race and Culture: Philosophy, Politics, and Poetics* (New York: Routledge, 1996) were essential, as was E. U. Essien-Udom's *Black Nationalism: A Search for an Identity in America* (Chicago: University of Chicago Press, 1962). Finally, additional context for the chapter was drawn from Jeffrey B. Perry's *Hubert Harrison: The Voice of Harlem Radicalism, 1883-1918* (New York: Columbia University Press, 2008); Mark R. Schneider's *"We Return Fighting": The Civil Rights Movement in the Jazz Age* (Boston: Northeastern University Press, 2002); Minkah Makalani's *In the Cause of Freedom: Radical Black Internationalism from Harlem to London, 1917-1939* (Chapel Hill: University of North Carolina Press, 2011); Kenneth Robert Janken's *White: The Biography of Walter White, Mr. NAACP* (New York: New Press, 2003); Walter White's *A Man Called White: The Autobiography of Walter White* (1948; rpt., Athens: University of Georgia Press, 1995); B. Joyce Ross's *J. E. Spingarn and the Rise of the NAACP*

(New York: Atheneum, 1972); James Weldon Johnson's *Along This Way: The Autobiography of James Weldon Johnson* (1933; rpt., New York: Da Capo, 2000); Eugene Levy's *James Weldon Johnson: Black Leader, Black Voice* (Chicago: University of Chicago Press, 1973); Jacqueline Anne Goggin, Carter G. Woodson, *A Life in Black History* (Baton Rouge: Louisiana State University Press, 1993); Pero Gaglo Dagbovie, *The Early Black History Movement, Carter G. Woodson, and Lorenzo Johnston Greene* (Urbana: University of Illinois Press, 2007); Irene Diggs's "Du Bois—Revolutionary Journalist Then and Now: Part I," *A Current Bibliography of African Affairs* 4, no. 2 (1971): 96; Mark Ellis's "'Closing Ranks' and 'Seeking Honors': W. E. B. Du Bois in World War I," *Journal of American History* 79, no. 1 (1992): 96–124; William Tuttle Jr.'s *Race Riot: Chicago in the Red Summer of 1919* (New York: Atheneum, 1970); Elliott Rudwick's *Race Riot at East St. Louis July 2, 1917* (Urbana: University of Illinois Press, 1982); Chad Louis Williams's *Torchbearers of Democracy: African American Soldiers in World War I Era* (Chapel Hill: University of North Carolina Press, 2010); and Theodore Kornweibel's two excellent books on the war era, *Seeing Red: Federal Campaigns against Black Militancy, 1919-1925* (Bloomington: Indiana University Press, 1998) and *Investigate Everything: Federal Efforts to Compel Black Loyalty During World War I* (Bloomington, IN: Indiana University Press, 2002).

CHAPTER 5

In addition to the biographies by Lewis, Marable, Rudwick, Wolters, Horne, and Rampersad and Du Bois's autobiographies *Dusk of Dawn* and *The Autobiography*, this chapter consulted his writings in *The Crisis* magazine; Herbert Aptheker's edited *Newspaper Columns, Vol. 1: 1945-1961* (White Plains, NY: Kraus-Thomson, 1986) and *Writings by W. E. B. Du Bois in Periodicals Edited by Others, Vol. 4: 1945-1961* (Millwood, NY: Kraus-Thomson, 1982); "A Negro Nation within the Nation," *Current History* 42 (1935): 265–70; "Does the Negro Need Separate Schools?" *Journal of Negro Education* 4, no. 3 (1935): 328–35; "Social Planning for the Negro, Past and Present," *Journal of Negro Education* 5, no. 1 (1936): 110–25; *Black Folk Then and Now: An Essay in the History and Sociology of the Negro Race* (1939; rpt. New York: Octagon Books, 1970); *Black Reconstruction* (1935; rpt., Millwood, NY: Kraus-Thomson, 1976); *Color and Democracy: Colonies and Peace* (New York: Harcourt Brace, 1945); *The World and Africa*

(Millwood, NY: Kraus-Thomson, 1976); and "The Negro and Social Recon-struction," in *Against Racism*.

Several books provide additional context for the period addressed in the chapter. Sullivan's *Lift Every Voice*; Janken's *White*; White's *A Man Called White*; Ross's *J. E. Spingarn and the Rise of the NAACP*; Eric Porter's *The Problem of the Future World: W. E. B. Du Bois and the Race Concept at Midcentury* (Durham, NC: Duke University Press, 2010); Gerald Horne's *Race Woman: The Lives of Shirley Graham Du Bois* (New York: New York University Press, 2000); Eben Miller's *Born Along the Color Line: The 1933 Amenia Conference and the Rise of a National Civil Rights Movement* (New York: Oxford University Press, 2012); Jonathan Scott Holloway's *Confront-ing the Veil: Abram Harris, Jr., E. Franklin Frazier, and Ralph Bunche, 1919-1941* (Chapel Hill: University of North Carolina Press, 2002); Eric Foner's "Black Reconstruction: An Introduction," *South Atlantic Quarterly* 112, no. 3 (2013): 409–18; Thomas C. Holt's "'A Story of Ordinary Human Beings': The Sources of Du Bois's Historical Imagination in *Black Recon-struction*," *South Atlantic Quarterly* 112, no. 3 (2013): 419–35; Jonathan B. Fenderson, "Evolving Conceptions of Pan-African Scholarship: W. E. B. Du Bois, Carter G. Woodson, and the 'Encyclopedia Africana,' 1909-1963," *Journal of African American History* 95, no. 1 (2010): 71–91; James T. Campbell, *Middle Passages: African American Journeys to Africa, 1787-2005* (New York: Penguin Press, 2006); and Robert Shogan's *Harry Truman and the Struggle for Racial Justice* (Lawrence: University Press of Kansas, 2012).

CHAPTER 6

In addition to the biographies by Lewis, Marable, Rudwick, Wolters, Horne, and Rampersad, and Du Bois's autobiographies *Dusk of Dawn* and *The Auto-biography*, this chapter consulted *In Battle for Peace: The Story of My 83rd Birthday, with Comment by Shirley Graham* (New York: Masses & Main-stream, 1952); *The Ordeal of Mansart* (New York: Mainstream Publishers, 1957); *Mansart Builds a School* (New York: Masses & Mainstream, 1959); *Worlds of Color* (New York: Mainstream Publishers, 1961); Herbert Apthek-er's edited *Writings by W. E. B. Du Bois in Periodicals Edited by Others, Vol. 4: 1945-1961*; and John Henrik Clarke, Esther Jackson, Ernest Kaiser, and J. H. O'Dell's edited *Black Titan: W. E. B. Du Bois; an Anthology* (Boston: Beacon Press, 1970).

Context for the Cold War era, anticolonialism, and the peace movement can be found in the following books: Murali Balaji's *The Professor and the Pupil: The Politics of W. E. B. Du Bois and Paul Robeson* (New York: Nation Books, 2007); Brenda Gayle Plummer's *Rising Wind: Black Americans and U.S. Foreign Affairs, 1935-1960* (Chapel Hill: University of North Carolina Press, 1996); Cedric Belfrage and James Aronson's *Something to Guard: The Stormy Life of the National Guardian, 1948-1967* (New York: Columbia University Press, 1978); Thomas Borstelmann's *The Cold War and the Color Line: American Race Relations in the Global Arena* (Cambridge, MA: Harvard University Press, 2001); Penny M. Von Eschen's *Race against Empire: Black Americans and Anticolonialism, 1937-1957* (Ithaca, NY: Cornell University Press, 1997); David Henry Anthony's *Max Yergan: Race Man, Internationalist, Cold Warrior* (New York: New York University Press, 2006); Martin B. Duberman's *Paul Robeson* (New York: Knopf, 1988); Lindsey R. Swindall's *Paul Robeson: A Life of Activism and Art* (New York: Rowman & Littlefield Publishers, 2013); and *The Path to the Greater, Freer, Truer World: Southern Civil Rights and Anticolonialism, 1937-1955* (Gainesville: University Press of Florida, 2014). Additional background and context for this chapter can be found in David Levering Lewis, Michael H. Nash, and Daniel J. Leab's edited *Red Activists and Black Freedom: James and Esther Jackson and the Long Civil Rights Revolution* (New York: Routledge, 2010); Gerald Meyer's *Vito Marcantonio: Radical Politician, 1902-1954* (Albany: State University of New York Press, 1989); Robbie Lieberman and Clarence Lang's edited *Anticommunism and the African American Freedom Movement: "Another Side of the Story"* (New York: Palgrave Macmillan, 2009); James T. Campbell, *Middle Passages: African American Journeys to Africa, 1787-2005* (New York: Penguin Press, 2006); and Kevin K. Gaines's *American Africans in Ghana: Black Expatriates and the Civil Rights Era* (Chapel Hill: University of North Carolina Press, 2006).

Index

Accra, Ghana, 1, 128
"An Address to the Nations of the World"
  (Du Bois, W. E. B.), 31
aestheticism, 31; in African civilizations,
  67–68; Harlem Renaissance, 81, 82, 83,
  101
Africa: "The African Roots of the War",
  68; artistic sensibility in civilizations
  of, 67–68; cultural heritage from, 29;
  Diaspora, 31, 66–67, 98; Du Bois, W.
  E. B., first visit to, 75; Du Bois, W. E.
  B., return to, 98; *Encyclopedia
  Africana*, 66, 98, 129; Ghana, 1, 128;
  The Horizon on, 29; independence from
  colonial rule, 64, 75; iron curtain
  between Europe and, 105; myth about,
  27; national independence movements,
  103; *The Negro* on, 66–68; slave trade
  from, 11–12, 13, 19–20; Universal
  African Legion, 76; *When Africa
  Awakes*, 72; *The World and Africa: An
  Inquiry into the Part Which Africa Has
  Played in World History*, 22, 105. *See
  also* Pan-African Conference; Pan-
  Africanism
African Methodist Episcopal (AME)
  Church, 18; in Boston riot, 48–49
"The African Roots of the War" (Du Bois,
  W. E. B.), 68
Afro-American Council, 42, 47, 53
Afro-American League, 29, 53

Allen, Ernest, Jr., 44
Allison, Andrew J., 101
All-Soviet Peace Conference, 114
AME. *See* African Methodist Episcopal
  Church
Amenia Conference, New York, 65–66
American Labor Party, 116–117, 117
American Missionary Association, 6, 23
American Negro Academy, Washington D.
  C.., 29
"The American Negro and Communism"
  (Du Bois, W. E. B.), 126
"*An Appeal to the World: A Statement on
  the Denial of Human Rights to
  Minorities in the Case of Citizens of
  Negro Descent in the United States of
  America and an Appeal to the United
  Nations for Redress*", 104
ancestry, of Du Bois, W. E. B., 4
anticolonialism, 103, 104, 105, 107, 111,
  113, 131
Aptheker, Herbert, 128
Arena, 20
Arnett, Benjamin W., 19
art, is propaganda, 82
Asia, 29, 103
"As the Crow Flies" (Du Bois, W. E. B.),
  112
"Atlanta Compromise" address
  (Washington), 36–37
Atlanta riot (1906), 33, 54, 54–55

145

Atlanta Studies (Du Bois, W. E. B.),
    25–28, 57, 100
Atlanta University, 23–25, 24; resignation
    from, 58; retired from, 102; second
    tenure at, 92–93, 95
The Atlanta University Publications (1896-
    1914)(Du Bois, W. E. B.), 25
Atlantic Monthly, 20
Austria, 15
The Autobiography (Du Bois, W. E. B.),
    123
The Autobiography of an Ex-Colored Man
    (Johnson, J. W.), 66
Azikiwe, Nnamdi, 128

Baker, Newton D., 70
Baker, Ray Stannard, 36, 37–38
Baldwin, James, 131
Baldwin, William Henry, 37, 42
Barber, J. Max, 52
Barnett, Ferdinand, 40, 42
Bass, Charlotta, 111
Bentley, C. C., 52
Berlin, University of, 14–15
Bethel Literary Historical Association,
    Washington D. C., 29
Bethune, Mary McLeod, 104
Bible of the Negro race, 46
The Birth of a Nation, 43
Bishop, Hutchins, 71
Bismarck, Otto von, 10–11
*Black Folk Then and Now: An Essay in the
    History and Sociology of the Negro
    Race* (Du Bois, W. E. B.), 98
black freedom movement, 98, 100
Black Nationalism, 76
*Black Reconstruction: An Essay toward a
    History of the Part Which Black Folk
    Played in the Attempt to Reconstruct
    Democracy in America, 1860-1880* (Du
    Bois, W. E. B.), 94
*Black Reconstruction: Black Folk Then
    and Now* (Du Bois, W. E. B.), 93,
    95–97
Black Star steamship line, 76
Blight, David W., 96
Boas, Franz, 63
Bond, Horace Mann, 1, 108
Bond, Julian, 1–2

Bontemps, Arna, 81
Booklover's Magazine, 48, 49
Boston Brahmins, 11
Boston riot (1903), 48–49
Bradford, George, 24
Braithwaite, Stanley, 81
Brawley, Benjamin G., 63
British Empire, 101. *See also* Europe;
    imperialism
Brooks, Gwendolyn, 81
Brown, Charlotte Hawkins, 120
Brown, John, 53–54, 57
Brownies Book, 74
Brownsville Affair (Texas), 54
Brown v. Board of Education, 124
Buchanan v. Worley, 74
Bunche, Ralph, 97, 111, 120
Burghardt, Mary (mother), 2, 3, 6
Byrnes, James F., 2

Cain, William E., 94
Calhoun, William P., 20
call-and-response tradition, 58
Calvinist ethics, 22
Canadian Peace Conference, 122
Capitalism, 95, 105, 107; calls
    Communism a crime, 129; as
    destructive force, 127
Caribbean, 75, 103
Carroll, Charles, 28
caste system, by color, 78
*The Caucasian and The Negro in the
    United States. They Must Separate. If
    Not, Then Extermination. A Proposed
    Solution: Colonization* (Calhoun), 20
Central America, 75
Chase, William Calvin, 62
Chesnutt, Charles, 63
Chicago, 36
China, 127
Chou Enlai, 127
Christian faith, 18
Civil Rights Act (1875), 8
Civil Rights Cases, 17
The Clansmen (Dixon), 43, 54
Clarke, Edward E., 29
close ranks, 102
"Close Ranks" (Du Bois, W. E. B.), 72–73;
    Garvey's criticism of, 77

Cold War, 104, 106, 112–115, 118–123
The College-Bred Negro (Du Bois, W. E. B.), 26
colonialism: African independence from, 64, 75; anti-, 103, 104, 105, 107, 111, 113, 131
Color and Democracy: Colonies and Peace (Du Bois, W. E. B.), 103
Committee of Twelve, 50, 53
Communism, 94, 104, 111, 126; as crime, 129. *See also* trial, of Du Bois, W. E. B.
Congregationalist Church, 7, 18
"Conservation of the Races", 66, 67
"The Conservation of the Races" (Du Bois, W. E. B.), 30–31
The Conservator, 40
Constitution League, 53
Consumers Cooperation, 129
cooperatives, economic, 94–95
corporate power, 127
Cotton States and International Exposition, Atlanta, 37
courage, 13, 35, 50
"Credo", 58
The Crisis: A Record of the Darker Races, 2, 58, 59, 60; black middle class readership, 61; future activists educated by, 64; on Garvey, 79–80; resignation from, 91–92; revolutionary nature of, 64; White, W., versus Du Bois, W. E. B., at, 87–91, 106–107
Cromwell, John Wesley, 29
Crummel, Alexander, 50
Cullen, Countee, 81
Cultural and Scientific Conference for World Peace, Paris, 112, 113
cultural pluralism, 30

Daniels, John, 47, 96
Dark Princess: A Romance (Du Bois, W. E. B.), 83
Darkwater: Voices from within the Veil (Du Bois, W. E. B.), 83
Davis, Jefferson, 12
Debs, Eugene, 94
de facto segregation, 4, 17, 91
de jure segregation, 4, 8, 17, 91
democracy, 111; as conceived in U. S., 11, 60, 107, 127, 132; is nonexistent in

America, 94, 102, 117; redefining, 114; World War I as fight for, 71–72
Democratic Party, 106–107
Depression, 83, 93, 94; racial hostilities sharpened by, 93
"The Descent of Dr. Du Bois" (Harrison, H.), 72
Diaspora, African, 31, 66–67, 98
Dickerson, Earl, 104
Diggs, Ellen Irene, 63
discipline, as charge to African America, 27
disenfranchisement laws, 34
Dixon, Thomas, 28, 43, 54
Domingo, Wilfred Adolphus, 76
double consciousness, 44–45
Douglass, Frederick, 37, 50
Douglass, Lewis, 54
Du Bois, Burghardt Gomer (son), 32, 38
Du Bois, Nina (wife), 19, 32, 38, 49, 87, 107, 114; as grandmother, 101; stays in New York, 93
Du Bois, William Edward Burghardt (W. E. B.), 3, 6, 12, 32, 71, 87, 117; *See also* specific topics
Du Bois, Yolanda (daughter), 49, 81, 93, 101
Dunning, William A., 96
Dusk of Dawn: An Essay Toward an Autobiography of a Race Concept (Du Bois, W. E. B.), 4, 37–38, 74, 80, 100–101, 123

"The Economic Aspects of Race Prejudice" (Du Bois, W. E. B.), 28
Einstein, Albert, 122
Elkin, Kyrle, 118
Encyclopedia Africana, 66, 98, 129
"The Enforcement of the Slave Trade Laws" (Du Bois, W. E. B.), 13
environmental influence, *The Philadelphia Negro* describing, 22
Europe, 13, 67; imperialist, 68; iron curtain between Africa and, 105; travels in, 15; wine, women, and song days in, 15

Farris, William, 46
Fauset, Jessie Redmond, 81
Fisk University, 6, 7–8, 9, 86

Fleming, Walter Lynwood, 96
Folkways (Sumner), 28
Following the Color Line (Baker, R. S.), 36
Forbes, George W., 41
Fortune, T. Thomas, 5, 34, 47, 50
Forum, 20
Fourteenth Amendment, 4
France, 4, 16, 68, 75, 129
Frazier, E. Franklin, 63, 77, 97, 108, 120
Freedmen's Bureau, 44
funeral/memorial, for Du Bois, W. E. B.,
    1–2, 131–132

Garrison, William Lloyd, 51
Garvey, Marcus, 2, 76; *The Crisis* on,
    79–80
Germany, University of Berlin days, 14–15
Ghana, 1, 128
*The Gift of Black Folk: Negroes in the
    Making of America* (Du Bois, W. E.
    B.), 83
Giles v. Harris (1903), 43
Gomer, Nina, 19
graduate school, 12, 12–13
Graham, D. A., 108
Graham, Shirley (second wife of Du Bois,
    W. E. B.), 108, 113, 116, 118, 120, 126
Grant, Ulysses S., 4
Great Barrington, Massachusetts, 2, 3, 4,
    87; high school graduation, 6
Grimké, Francis James, 29
The Guardian, 41
Guinn v. U. S., 74
Gunner, Byron, 72
Gypsies, 15

Hall, Gus, 129
Hancock, Gordon B., 122
Harcourt, Brace and Company, 123
Harlem, Manhattan, 101, 103–104, 116,
    120; Garvey's headquarters in, 76, 79
Harlem Renaissance, 81, 83, 101; Du Bois,
    W. E. B., on aesthetics, 82
Harper's Ferry, West Virginia, 53–54
Harper's Weekly, 20
Harris, Abram L., 94
Harrison, Hubert, 72
Hart, Albert Bushnell, 11–12, 20

Harvard College, 11, 11–13; graduation,
    12; inability to attend, 7
Hayes, Rutherford B., 13
Herndon, Angelo, 94
Hershaw, Lafayette, 29
high school graduation, 6
Hitlers in America, 101
Home University Library series, 66
Hope, John, 40, 92–93
"Hopeful Signs for the Negro" (Du Bois,
    W. E. B.), 41
The Horizon: A Journal of the Color Line,
    29
Hose, Sam, 33
House Committee of Foreign Affairs, 114
How the Other Half Lives (Riis), 36
Hudson, Hosea, 94
Hughes, Langston, 2, 63, 81, 121
Human Rights Commission, United
    Nations, 104
Hunton, Alphaeus, 103, 111, 129
Hurston, Zora Neale, 63, 81

imperialism, 68, 74, 94–95, 103–105
*In Battle for Peace: The Story of My 83rd
    Birthday, with Comment by Shirley
    Graham* (Du Bois, W. E. B.), 116
Independent, 34
intermarriage, 8
Irish immigrants, 5
iron curtain, 105

Jackson, James E., 2
Jacques-Garvey, Amy, 104
James, William, 11
Japan, 101
Jemison, D. W., 104
Jews, 15
Jim Crow system, 8–9, 10, 37; radicalized
    political outlook in response to, 34;
    reign of terror accompanying, 17; *The
    Souls of Black Folk* as testament
    against, 43
Johnson, Andrew, 4
Johnson, Charles S., 81, 100, 121
Johnson, Fenton, 63
Johnson, James Weldon, 63, 66, 71, 87; on
    impact of *The Souls of Black Folk*, 46;
    NAACP fieldwork by, 23

Johnson, Mordecai, 120
Johnson, Wallace, 104
The Jungle (Sinclair), 35–36
Justice Department, U. S., Du Bois, W. E.
B., on trial, 120–122

Kenyatta, Jomo, 104
Khrushchev, Nikita, 127
Killens, John Oliver, 131
King, Martin Luther, Jr., 124, 132
Konvitz, Milton, 104
Ku Klux Klan, 43, 73, 78

labor rights. *See* working classes
"Last Message to the World" (Du Bois, W.
E. B.), 132
The Leopard's Spots (Dixon), 28, 43
Lewis, David Levering, 9, 29, 31, 38; on
Du Boisian intellectual idealism, 102;
on *The Souls of Black Folk*, 42
"A Litany of Atlanta" (Du Bois, W. E. B.),
33
Locke, Alain, 108, 120
Logan, Rayford W., 100, 104
Lowell, James Russell, 60
lynching, 17–18, 27, 37, 63, 64;
Depression era, 93; without fear of
punishment, 43; first-hand account, 74;
NAACP anti-, parade, 71; social control
through, 20; after World War I, 73
"The Lynching Industry" (Wells-Barnett),
64

Macneal, Arthur C., 2
Manchester, England, 103
Manley, Norman, 104
Mao Tse-tung, 127
Marable, Manning, 22, 29
Marbach, Dora, 13
Marcantonio, Vito, 116
March on Washington for Jobs and
Freedom (1963), 1, 130
Marx, Karl, 94
Marxists, 94
master's thesis, 13
McCarran Act (Subversive Activities
Control Act)(1950), 122, 128
McClurg, A. C., 42
McGhee, F. L., 52

McGrath, J. Howard, 112
McGuire, Matthew F., 121–122
McKay, Claude, 81
Mencken, H. L., 63
Miller, Kelly, 29, 50
Ming, William R., 104
Montgomery, Winfield, 38
The Moon Illustrated Weekly, 28
Moore, Fred, 65–66
Moos, Elizabeth, 118
Morehouse, Henry, 39
Morehouse College, Atlanta, 39
Morgan, Clement, 48
muckraking, investigative, 35–36
Murray, Freeman, 29
myths, challenged, 26, 27, 30

NAACP. *See* National Association for the
Advancement of Colored People
Nail, Jack, 71
Naples, Italy, 15
Nashville, Tennessee, 7–10
The Nation, 20
National Association for the Advancement
of Colored People (NAACP), 56,
59–60, 71, 83; Amenia Conference
impacting, 65–66; *The Crisis* and, 61;
Garvey on, 79; return to, as director of
special research, 103
National Equal Rights League, 72
National Negro Business League, 29, 48
nation within a nation, 97
The Negro (Du Bois, W. E. B.), 66–68
*The Negro, A Menace to American
Civilization* (Shufeldt), 28
The Negro a Beast; Or In the Image of God
(Carroll), 28
"The Negro and Crime" (Du Bois, W. E.
B.), 28
"The Negro and Social Reconstruction"
(Du Bois, W. E. B.), 93
The Negro Artisan (Du Bois, W. E. B.), 26
The Negro Common School (Du Bois, W.
E. B.), 26
Negro Cooperative Guild, 86
"The Negroes of Farmville, Virginia; A
Social Study" (Du Bois, W. E. B.), 28
"The Negro in the Black Belt" (Du Bois,
W. E. B.), 28

"The Negro Landholders of Georgia" (Du
  Bois, W. E. B.), 28
"Negro Literacy" (Du Bois, W. E. B.), 57
"A Negro Nation within a Nation" (Du
  Bois, W. E. B.), 97
Negro Press Organization, 29
The Negro Program, 22–23, 28
Negro World, 76
New Bedford, Massachusetts, 7
New Negro, 81, 82
New York Globe, 5
Niagara Falls Movement, 52–54
Nkrumah, Fathia Rizk, 130
Nkrumah, Kwame, 104, 128, 130
nonviolence, 124, 132
North American Review, 20

"Of Booker T. Washington and Others"
  (Du Bois, W. E. B.), 47
Ogden, Robert C., 49
Oklahoma, 74
Outlook, 20, 26
Ovington, Mary White, 120
Owen, Chandler, 72, 76

Padmore, George, 103–104
Pan-African Conference, 31; Belgium, 76;
  Manchester, 103–104
Pan-Africanism, 31, 64, 75, 76; father of,
  104; working classes unified with, 68,
  94–95
parks, 43
"Parting the Ways" (Du Bois, W. E. B.), 50
passport, revoked, 124, 125–126
Payne, Daniel Alexander, 18, 50
peace: All-Soviet Peace Conference, 114;
  In Battle for Peace, 116; Canadian
  Peace Conference, 122; *Color of
  Democracy: Colonies and Peace*, 103;
  Cultural and Scientific Conference for
  World Peace, Paris, 112, 113; PIC, 114,
  115–116, 118; Versailles Peace
  Conference, 75; world, 102, 112, 113,
  116, 120
Peace Information Center (PIC), 114,
  115–116, 118
Pearl Harbor, 101
Perry, Leslie S., 104
Philadelphia, 21–23

The Philadelphia Negro (Du Bois, W. E.
  B.), 22–23
philosophy major, at Harvard, 11–13
*Phylon: A Quarterly Review of Race and
  Culture* (Du Bois, W. E. B.), 93, 100
Pickens, William, 63
Pittsburgh Courier, 131
Plessy v. Ferguson (1896), 17, 48
Poitier, Sidney, 131
Popular Science Monthly, 20
Powell, Adam Clayton, Jr., 104
Prattis, P. L., 131
"The Present Crisis" (Lowell), 60
press, unsubsidized, 52
progressivism, 20, 22, 35–36, 118; as
  failure in U. S., 129
propaganda journalism, 29, 82

The Quest of the Silver Fleece (Du Bois,
  W. E. B.), 82

"Race Friction between Black and White"
  (Du Bois, W. E. B.), 28
race purity, 78
racial pride, 21, 26, 27, 76, 131
railway cars, 17, 43
Randolph, A. Philip, 72
rape myth, challenged, 27
"Reconstruction and Its Benefits" (Du
  Bois, W. E. B.), 57
religious revivalism, 18
respectability, through manners and
  morality, 5, 22, 27, 116
restaurants, 43
Riis, Jacob, 36
Robeson, Paul, 103, 108, 111, 113, 120
Roosevelt, Eleanor, 104
Roosevelt, Theodore, 37
Rudwick, Elliott, 26, 62
Ruffin, George Lewis, 11
Ruffin, Josephine, 11

Santayana, George, 11
Scandinavia, 129
Scarborough, William S., 29
Schmoller, Gustav, 14, 20
Schomburg, Arthur, 63
Schuyler, George S., 59, 97, 101
Secure These Rights, 106

sedition accusation, 2. *See also* trial, of Du Bois, W. E. B.

segregation: black community response to, 21; Du Bois, W. E. B., favoring, 97; Niagara Falls Movement on, 52; *Plessy v. Ferguson*, 48; sanctioned by science, law, and public opinion, 61; *United States v. Stanley*, 17; veil of, 43, 45, 83; *Williams v. Mississippi*, 48

self-reliance, 21, 27, 94–95

self-respect, 22

self-segregation, 86–87, 101

sharecroppers, 43, 94

Shufeldt, Robert W., 28

Silver, Abba Hillel, 120

Simon, Abbott, 118

Sinclair, Upton, 35–36

Sinclair, William, 60

Slater Fund for the Education of Negroes, 13

slave trade, 11–12, 13, 19–20

Smith, Harry C., 40

Social Darwinism, 20

socialism, 94, 111, 127

"Sociology Hesitant" (Du Bois, W. E. B.), 28

solidarity, 21, 30, 94

Soloff, Sylvia, 118

"The Sorcery of Color" (Du Bois, W. E. B.), 93

The Souls of Black Folk: Essays and Sketches (Du Bois, W. E. B.), 42–43, 45; blacks as asset to national tradition, 45; 'double consciousness' idea, 44–45; first racial consciousness, 5; impact of, 1; as political Bible, 46; as reform literature, 43; on Washington, B. T., 46

South America, 75

South Carolina, 2

Southern History Association Publications, 26

Southern Negro Youth Conference, 94

Soviet Union, 114, 127

Spingarn, Arthur, 107, 120

Spingarn, Joel E., 62, 65, 70, 87, 88, 120; birthday party for Du Bois, W. E. B., 69–70

spiritual isolation, 7

Staatswissenschaften, 14

Statue of Liberty, 16

Stevens, Thaddeus, 2–4

Streator, George, 97

Student Nonviolent Coordinating Committee, 1–2

student seminars, at home of Du Bois, W. E. B., 25

"The Study of the Negro Problem" (Du Bois, W. E. B.), 28

Subversive Activities Control Act (McCarran Act)(1950), 122, 128

Sumner, William Graham, 28

The Suppression of the African Slave Trade to the United States of America, 1638-1870 (Du Bois, W. E. B.), 11–12, 19–20

Switzerland, 15

Talented Tenth theory, 39

tenant's rights, 94

Terrell, Mary Church, 38, 120

Terrell, Robert H., 38

theaters, 43

"The Conservation of the Races", 31

The World and Africa: An Inquiry into Which Africa Has Played in World History (Du Bois, W. E. B.), 32, 105

Till, Emmett, 64

trans-Atlantic slave trade, 11–12, 13, 19–20

transnationalism, 30

Treitschke, Henrich von, 14

trial, of Du Bois, W. E. B., 121–122; aftermath of, 122–123; passport revoked, 124, 125–126; preparation for, 120–121

Trotter, William Monroe, 40–41, 52, 60

Truman, Harry, 106, 107, 121–122

Turner, Nat, 58

Tuskegee Institute, Alabama, 18, 24, 36, 42; 1902 conference at, 28; as "Tuskegee Machine", 39, 46, 47. *See also* Washington, Booker T.

unemployment, 1, 73, 94, 130; during Depression, 93; jeopardizing one's job for higher principle, 116

UNIA. *See* Universal Negro Improvement Association

United Nations, 103
United States v. Stanley (1883), 17
Universal African Legion, 76
Universal Negro Improvement Association
   (UNIA), 2, 76–77
Universal Races Conference, London
   (1911), 66
University of Berlin, 14–15
University of Pennsylvania, 19
Up from Slavery (Washington, B. T.), 41
Urban League, 81

Van Vechten, Carl, 82
veil, as trope, 43, 45, 83
Venice, Italy, 15
Versailles Peace Conference, 75
Villard, Oswald Garrison, 51, 61, 63
Voice of the Negro, 52
voting rights, 34, 52; *Giles v. Harris*, 43;
   for women, 64

Waco (Texas) lynching (1916), 64
Wagner, Adolf, 14
Walling, William English, 60
Walters, Alexander, 56, 60
Washington, Booker T., 19, 34, 39, 46, 47,
   48; "Atlanta Compromise" address,
   36–37; on Atlanta riot, 55; Baker, R. S.,
   characterization of, 37–38; Du Bois, W.
   E. B., and, 28, 37–38, 38–40; Du Bois,
   W. E. B., break with, 48–57; Du Bois,
   W. E. B.,"Parting the Ways" about, 50;
   early years, 36; *The Horizon* on, 29;
   obituary for, 65; "Of Booker T.
   Washington and Others", 47; public
   philosophy of, 37; *The Souls of Black
   Folk: Essays and Sketches* about, 46;
   Southern conditions requiring
   compromise, 41, 49. *See also* Tuskegee
   Institute, Alabama
Washington, Jesse, 64
Weber, Max, 14
Wells-Barnett, Ida B., 27, 60; appreciation
   for *The Souls of Black Folk*, 42; "The
   Lynching Industry", 64
When Africa Awakes (Harrison, H.), 72
White, Walter, 63; Du Bois, W. E. B., and,
   87–91, 106–107; fear of Communist
   Party connection, 104

white Americans: Atlanta riot, 33, 54,
   54–55; Boston riot, 48–49; *The
   Caucasian and The Negro in the United
   States. They Must Separate. If Not,
   Then Extermination. A Proposed
   Solution: Colonization*, 20; *The Crisis*
   as "must" read for, 59; everyday
   violence of, 8–9; failed progressivism,
   129; imperialist politics, 68, 74; myths
   about Africans, 26, 27, 30; suppressed
   evidence, misquoted authority,
   deliberate lies by, 57; supremacist
   politics, 17, 20–21, 31. *See also*
   Capitalism; democracy; Jim Crow
   system; lynching
Wilberforce University, 18
Wilkins, Roy, 1, 76, 125, 130
Williams, Arnett, 101
Williams, Du Bois (grandson of Du Bois,
   W. E. B.), 101
Williams, Fannie Barrier, 42
Williams, Henry Sylvester, 31
Williams, Mangus, 104
Williams, Robert, 124
Williams, S. Laing, 42
Williams v. Mississippi (1898), 48
Wilson, Woodrow, 70, 93; Du Bois, W. E.
   B., endorses, 94
wine, women, and song, 15
Woodson, Carter G., 68, 73, 98, 100
Work, Monroe, 42
work ethic, 5, 22, 88
working classes: American Labor Party,
   116–117, 117; black, in wartime
   economy, 73; black and white unified,
   97; labor rights, 64; progressivism
   impacting, 35–36; represented in
   Atlanta Studies, 26; unemployment
   during Depression, 93; world-wide, 68,
   94–95
*The World and Africa: An Inquiry into the
   Part Which Africa Has Played in World
   History* (Du Bois, W. E. B.), 22, 105
world peace, 102, 116, 120; Cultural and
   Scientific Conference for World Peace,
   Paris, 112, 113
World War I: "The African Roots of the
   War", 68; agricultural price supports
   lifted after, 93; "Close Ranks", 72–73,

77; as fight for democracy, 71–72; first your Country, then your Rights, 73; lynching after, 73; U. S. enters, 70; Versailles Peace Conference, 75; white imperialism resulting in, 68
World War II, 93, 98, 101

Yergan, Max, 103, 112

Zionism, black, 31
Zionist Organization of America, 120

About the Author

Shawn Leigh Alexander is associate professor and graduate director of African and African American Studies and director of the Langston Hughes Center at the University of Kansas, where he specializes in African American social and intellectual history of the nineteenth and twentieth centuries. The author of *An Army of Lions: The Struggle for Civil Rights before the NAACP*, he has also edited an anthology of T. Thomas Fortune's writings, *T. Thomas Fortune, the Afro-American Agitator*; a collection on the racial violence after the Civil War, *Reconstruction Violence and the Ku Klux Klan Hearings*; and has written the introduction to a reprint of William Sinclair's classic 1905 study, *The Aftermath of Slavery: A Study of the Condition and Environment of the American Negro*. He has also authored many scholarly articles and book chapters on early African American civil rights activity and black intellectual history.